ADDICT BEHIND OUR BEDROOM DOOR

A Mother's Journey Through Her Child's Addiction:
Love, Fear, Struggle and Hope

By

D.L. WILSON

www.DLWilsonWrites.com

PRAISE FOR
ADDICT
BEHIND OUR BEDROOM DOOR

"After more than two decades as a Social Worker dedicated to facilitating change for individuals, families, and systems, I can speak to the epic depths of how mental illness and addiction can take over someone's life. The convergence of both often creates a personal house of cards with the slightest shift resulting in an avalanche of total devastation. This is trauma. This is life.

"D.L. Wilson's heartbreaking account of parenting her daughter Bianca, the subsequent waves of grief and loss, and her meaningful drive to understand her family's tragedy is a must read for interested parents, educators, and professionals."

Matthew G. Doyle, LICSW
Founding Director Castle Hill Counseling & Consulting, Inc.

"As a high school counselor in New Hampshire, ranked 2nd in the U.S. in opiate deaths, I have spent the past twenty years working closely with students and families through addiction and health issues, and I found 'Addict Behind Our Bedroom Door' to be an eye-opening, vividly written, breathtaking account for families looking for reassurance of what to do when mental health issues and drugs strike your family.

"Author D.L. Wilson pulls no punches in her detailed account in the heartbreaking story of raising her daughter through her childhood battles with addiction and mental illness. In this raw and personal story, may you find solace that the love and hope of family can be enough to survive your child's addiction."

John G. Webb, M.Ed
New Hampshire School Counselor
of the Year, 2018

"'Addict Behind Our Bedroom Door' is a gritty and complex look into the complicated world of both mental illness and substance abuse, as told by a loving mother who lived through her daughter's lifetime battle with one, the other, or both. If the reader has lived with such crises, the book is very familiar. If not, the book is very educational and should help the uninformed to develop empathy for those who must travel this highway.

"I applaud D.L. Wilson for opening up her life and allowing us inside, as we'll all come away with a much better understanding of an enormous national tragedy and crisis of epic proportions."

Chief Mark K. Leahy (Ret.)
Executive Director Massachusetts Chiefs of Police Association, Grafton, MA

"This book is a true testament to other families that they can survive addiction. 'Addict Behind Our Bedroom Door' provides insight on the resources available and how important follow-up is after initial treatment. Although you may have no control over the drug controlled addict, you have control of yourself.

"I read the entire book in one night. Could not put it down."

Detective Darlene Prinz
Beverly Police Department

"Riveting...heartbreaking...and compelling. A testament to the strength of a mother's love, the strongest and most unrelenting of all loves."

Paula Burnett DNP, RN, CNE.
Assistant Professor School of Nursing Salem State University

"As a parent of an opioid user in recovery, our world is isolated. When it's over, you can start to get a true perspective on what has happened. Until then, it's just chaos. This book provides useful insight to support your loved one without enabling them or the disease. Will help you get a handle on what is loving vs. enabling. A reminder not to blame yourself. Love yourself first."

Beth White

3

"A raw and powerful account of a mother's journey to save her daughter from the demons of mental illness complicated by the devastating impact of addiction. A first-hand heartfelt walk through the challenges of navigating the mental health system, insurance companies and available resources while struggling to find the fine line balance between trust, safety and enabling. This is a must read for parents to know that there is no blame or shame in asking for help as they do not have to be alone in their fight."

Karen J. Wilk
Education and Clinical Consultant

"The unvarnished window into mental illness and heroin addiction that D.L. Wilson gives in 'Addict Behind Our Bedroom Door' is almost too heartbreaking to bear. Reading this first-hand account from a mother in grief is a bit like the experience of tough love itself: It forces the reader to face and comprehend the gravity of this health epidemic and the tragic consequences it has in the lives of ordinary people we know and love. It is only the persistent, unconditional and sacrificial love that she and her husband, Karl, had for their daughter - and continue to have for her - which redeems this story of tremendous loss. That they are able to share their story so openly is a testament not only to their courage and strength as a family, but to their faith, which always holds out hope that what's lost can be found again - whether here or in the life to come."

The Rev. Jonathan R. Niketh
Pastor, First Lutheran Church, Lynn, MA

"This book, 'Addict Behind Our Bedroom Door,' is a must read for anyone who has experienced living with a loved one with a dual diagnosis of mental illness and addiction. D.L. Wilson writes from the heart an honest and raw account of her family's love for their daughter and their efforts to help her."

Edward Lyons
M.Ed. LMHC

THIS BOOK WILL HELP YOU TO:

- Understand what it is like to live with an addict.

- Give yourself permission to try to live your life
  in spite of your loved one's addiction.

- Remove the shame and guilt from parenting
  a child with addiction.

- Take away the shame and guilt from loving an addict.

- Understand what siblings, grandparents and friends
  should know when offering help and advice.

- Realize that you are doing the best you can; their
  addiction is NOT your fault.

- Set boundaries to reclaim your safety and peace.

- Recognize that it is OK to ask for help.

- Use resources to get help for you, your family
  and the addict.

- Allow imperfections when dealing with addiction.

- Accept that your efforts may not be enough to
  save the addict.

- Hear the promise of hope, love and acceptance
  in the face of overwhelming loss.

Published by New Mark Press.
April 2018

Cover and Book Design
Ellyn Olson

ISBN: 978-0-9765241-2-0

CONTENTS

CONTENTS *continued*

I dedicate this book to
my loving husband, Karl.

Thank you for traveling with me on this journey
and never giving up hope or losing faith.

ACKNOWLEDGEMENTS

I wrote this book to bear witness to the trauma that Bianca experienced and the years we endured trying to help her. It was a rough and messy process. The memories threatened to engulf me when the mental illness and addiction wounds were opened once again.

Thank you to my editor, Gail Lowe. You honored our story and made the book sparkle with your attention to detail and editing expertise. My book was safe in your hands.

Everyone needs a friend and I am lucky to have several. Judy was by my side throughout our ordeal and kept me grounded with her wisdom and concern for our safety. Candi never judged our family and always accepted Bianca as a child worthy of love. Pat helped me carry the weight of a mother's grief and gave me a reason to get up every morning and go to work. Dee Dee rescued me with her secret chicken soup recipe when I couldn't eat and Sandra shared a safe place where friendship is sacred.

I want to acknowledge my wonderful family. You suffered with us, helping but helpless to stop Bianca's path of destruction. I couldn't have survived without your unwavering support and love. I am so grateful that you are in my life.

To Scott, you breathed life into this book with your vault of publishing and marketing knowledge. Thank you for your patience when grief stopped my writing in its tracks.

Thank you for always being there and understanding that sometimes there are no words.

Matthew G. Doyle, LICSW and Founding Director of Castle Hill Counseling and Consulting has been our counselor for years. He provided safe space and was a voice of reason in the midst of chaos, always reassuring us that we were doing a good job. Matt is a trusted confidant and family friend. The Beverly Public School system and Karen Wilk, the Out of District Special Education Coordinator gave Bianca every resource to help her succeed academically. They coordinated her Individualized Education Plan for twelve years at great expense, and we are very grateful for that support. The Beverly Police deserve much praise as well. They were always on call and showed up to help in every crisis with strength, compassion and sound advice. Thank you.

Finally, I want to give a special acknowledgement to our sons, Michael and Stephen. You lived this nightmare too. I pray that this book will ease some of the pain that you carry and help you understand how Bianca's illness affected us all. I am so blessed to be your mother and I thank God every day for you. I love you.

D. L. Wilson
DLWilsonWrites.com

INTRODUCTION

Our daughter, Bianca Lynn Wilson, came into our lives through the Massachusetts Department of Children and Families (DCF) in May of 1996.

Bianca was 25 months old. This bouncy, temperamental, exuberant, adorable, smart, funny toddler stole our hearts. It didn't matter that she had Dominican Republic origins and brown skin. It didn't matter that she had entered the world through another woman and was removed from her birth family because of neglect. We claimed her as our own. Our love was thicker than blood ties, and we thought it could overcome any obstacle. It never occurred to us that she would be consumed by her biology and that all of our love, caring and support could not make a difference in the end.

On the first day that we met, Bianca climbed into my lap, snuggled into a tight ball and stuck her thumb in her mouth. She looked up at me and declared, "Mama." It was the first word she spoke and it melted my heart. I fell in love with this toddler and loved her unconditionally. Adoption brought us together as mother and daughter. My heart soared when she was happy and cried when she was sad. Our love was as strong as any biological relationship between parent and child. Motherhood is the proudest accomplishment of my life, and I am humbled to have been given this opportunity.

Our relationship was not always smooth or easy. Like a harsh professor, Bianca tested me to the limits of my endurance. I went to places that I did not know existed. During the teenage years I was under a constant barrage of abuse from her mental illness and addiction. The stress almost broke me, and yet I managed to put one foot in front of the other and kept my family, my marriage and my sanity intact. I was forced to set limits with excruciating consequences. I had to admit that I could not help her anymore and agreed to commit her to a psychiatric hospital and residential treatment center when she was 14. This act removed her from our home and fractured our family. Although it gave us peace, we were changed forever. I was forced to choose between unconditional versus tough love and file felony charges, leaving her with a permanent criminal record when she stole my credit card. I weighed this decision against the need to self preserve after she repeatedly robbed our household and brought illegal activity through our doors. I knew this would render her homeless, but I had to let her go so I could be safe and reclaim the sanctity of my home. Balancing these polarities was hard when living in the avalanche of adolescence, mental illness, trauma and addiction.

I am not sure how I survived. My strong faith in God is the

lifeline that kept me from sinking. Through Him I received the strength to live when I didn't think I could make it through another day. My husband, Karl, also deserves praise and thanks. He was and is a rock of support to me and our family. Even though we were going through this nightmare together, he never stopped loving me and worked by my side in partnership to keep our family afloat. What we experienced was excruciating. I watched, helpless, as our daughter self-destructed in front of my eyes. I was powerless to save her from the ravages of mental illness and its aftermath. I tried hard but I did not always do well. There were many times when I was overwhelmed with the nightmare we were living. Our distress was on display for everyone to watch: Police cars and ambulances in our yard, phone calls at work coupled with Bianca's inability to behave in public all drew attention to our plight. There was no hiding the raw reality of mental illness. It was not pretty and there was no curb appeal or race for the cure to lean on. I was exhausted and at times felt as if it would never end. My health suffered. I developed high blood pressure, gained weight and suffered from insomnia. I was constantly anxious and afraid while waiting for the next bad thing to happen, which usually did. If not for Karl and my sons, I would have felt so alone.

Bianca was fortunate to have dedicated professionals working hard to help her. Police, probation officers, counselors, psychiatrists, pediatricians, nurses, school principals, teachers, Special Educator coordinators, social workers, school counselors, friends, family, clergy, attorneys, judges, mental health crisis workers, emergency medical technicians, neighbors, co-workers and local and state agencies all worked on her behalf. Collectively, they spent thousands of hours over many years working to stabilize and help Bianca get well.

I also had a responsibility to our daughter. I had to set aside my pride and admit that we needed help. I had to navigate the "system" and learn what resources were available. All this took hard work, time and energy. I searched the Internet, asked lots of questions, sought the counsel of professionals and worked side by side with Karl. We went to countless meetings and appointments and made lots of calls and e-mails. I took detailed notes of everything that happened. I made copies and communicated these "memos to memory" to the people who were helping us. I could never remove the 24-hour responsibility for Bianca's safety and my accountability at work in addition to the physical and emotional demands of the family. I had to function on limited, interrupted sleep, and I could not rest at home because of the chaos. Even though it was one more thing to do, this documentation as well as the support of Bianca's team of professionals, enabled us to get the help our daughter desperately needed.

I wrote this book to chronicle the journey we took with our daughter. Our story is about mental illness and the chaos left in its wake. It is also about survival. It is a testimony to all that we endured. In writing this book, I resurrected a flood of memories that bear witness to the love, resilience and strength that we shared while living in the throes of mental illness and addiction.

I do not know if our efforts were enough, and I wonder if we did everything that we should have. Would it have made a difference in the end? What I do know without a doubt is that we tried to do our best every day. We never gave up on our daughter and never gave up hope.

chapter **1**

RED FLAGS

Parenting does not come with a road map.

For me, motherhood began in a less than typical fashion when we adopted our children. Although the circumstances by which they came into our lives were different from most families, we loved, accepted and rejoiced in the gift that parenting brought. Overjoyed and delighted, the early years of raising children were active, messy, exhausting, memorable and fun. We were filled with love for our children and exuberance for the life we shared as a young family. It was a wonderful time.

If there were warning signs of what was to come, I did not see them. If I was alarmed when a behavior or event surfaced, I did not give it much thought. After all, I was learning how to be a parent on the job. Tantrums, sibling rivalry, defiance and occasional stealing were attributed to the effects of early disruption. I was aware of how separation, loss, trauma and grief seared the psyche of an adopted child. As an adoptee myself, I understand how it feels to be different in a family even when surrounded by much love. I felt I could make a difference given my unique perspective and my deep love for our children. Sadly, some things cannot be erased, even with the best parenting and unconditional love.

In order to gain a better perspective of where this story begins, I will give you a brief overview of our family. My husband, Karl, and I were married in 1982 after meeting in and dating through college. I am a registered nurse and Karl is vice president of a bank. We shared the love of children and both wanted to start a family right away. I was pregnant within 18 months, but sadly lost the pregnancy and suffered seven more miscarriages in the following years. In 1990, we began adoption preparations. This was a natural next step, and Karl and I eagerly waited for a placement. Our firstborn son, Michael, entered our lives in 1992 through an open adoption. His birth mother, Deanna, and I had a close relationship that was important to us both and supported Michael's identity as he grew. Our marriage was strong and we were surrounded with a loving family, a circle of close friends and enjoyed active involvement in our church and community. Our finances were sound. I was able to be at home with Michael, while working weekends and completing my graduate degree part-time. Karl and I both wanted more children and began inquiries into the Department of Social Services (DSS) to explore adoption options through this agency.

Karl and I wanted to adopt more children, but the cost of a private adoption was prohibitive as I was a stay-at-home mother working weekends part-time. We learned that DSS adoptions were "free" for Massachusetts residents and were impressed with the training, services, programs and level of support that was available. We immediately began parenting sessions and completed the adoption home study within six months. Karl and I were excited about the home study and eager to expand our family. We were especially interested in adopting siblings but did not restrict the selection based on gender or race. Six months later we received the much anticipated phone call from our social worker.

"We have two babies for you!" she said. Our youngest son, Stephen, was eight weeks old and our daughter, Bianca, was 25 months. Overnight, we went from a family of three to a family of five. We now had three beautiful and healthy children. Life was exhilarating and exhausting at the same time. We were overjoyed and confident that with love and commitment we could handle anything that came our way.

"Bianca has temper tantrums and holds her breath," the social worker told us. I can handle this, I thought. But it was more than I expected: Head banging, riotous screaming, turning blue and frequent tantrums lasting for 20 minutes were usually triggered by the word "no." After the screams subsided, Bianca was limp and exhausted. I was, too.

"Mommy is it okay now?" three year-old Michael would ask. Stephen would sit quietly in his infant seat, sucking his thumb and waiting for the storm to pass. I didn't know how to avoid or stop the raging, so I did what every mother does - I held her close and told her I loved her.

I was trying to keep up with three little ones, two of them in diapers. I did a pretty good job managing to get the children on a schedule and work with the DSS adoption team to finalize the placement. Bianca spoke Spanish and, as a result, had mild speech delays. We enrolled her in the Head Start program with a Speech Language Pathologist. Bianca loved toddler activities: Blocks, books, balls and plenty of play time. She enjoyed games of "peek-a-boo" and "pat-a-cake" and dropping objects into containers. There was much thumb sucking and she loved to cuddle for stories. Life settled into a daily routine that was structured and simple. The result was a stable environment for everyone. Her toddler tantrums eventually subsided by the end of the year and coincided with the adoption finalization. Bianca was attending preschool two days a week and continued to make significant speech and developmental gains. She was able to share toys with other children and hear the word "no" without too much fuss. The winter ushered in the usual succession of colds, ear infections and the flu. I managed the daily demands of parenting with careful note-keeping for each child. This organization was extremely helpful, especially during pediatrician visits. We were a young, active family and all was well.

In the fall of 1997, at the age of three, Bianca enrolled in a private pre-school. The staff was not prepared for Bianca's energy. She had difficulty focusing, was in constant motion and easily distracted. Some mothers kept their distance because of her rambunctiousness. The teachers worked hard to make the school experience successful, but there were difficulties because of their limited exposure to hyperactive children with behavior challenges. One morning, I received a call from the school. A teacher reported that Bianca had used the word "vagina" in class. The director said that this was inappropriate language for a three-year-old. They questioned where she learned it and, furthermore, were considering reporting us to DCF. The threat of a DCF investigation was shocking. As adoptive parents, we received extensive training and scrutiny from DCF; they had endorsed us to parent these children. That we were accused of inappropriate parenting, sexual misconduct and threatened with an investigation from the same agency that placed the children into our home was incredible. The school was following their prescriptive guidelines but misread our situation and misapplied their rule, which was unfair and hurtful. I arranged a meeting with the school director and explained that Bianca had seen her brother's penis and was curious as to why she did not have one. I taught Bianca the correct word for her equivalent part and introduced the topic of privacy. The misunderstanding was corrected, and we appreciated each other's point of view. The teachers took more time to understand Bianca and her challenges. They attended workshops the following summer to learn how to manage hyperactive children with behavioral issues.

Bianca had a habit of "finding" things. She noticed everything and would pocket candy from display cases, coins on the sidewalk and even other children's toys. She was so fast I often did not see her do it. She took a diamond bracelet from a neighbor during a carpool pickup, quietly slipping it into her backpack.

The teachers discovered the jewelry during the course of the day and greeted me at school pick-up with the exclamation, "We found your diamond bracelet." I confessed that I did not own a diamond bracelet. I was embarrassed, but fortunately the bracelet was returned with a sincere apology. The carpool and future play dates ended with that nice family. In retrospect, perhaps I should have cautioned my friend about Bianca's worldview. I should have kept a closer watch and not let her out of my sight. It was too late and recriminations were of no help. Bianca had taken jewelry out of my jewelry box before, bringing pieces to the playground to play with. When admonished that she was not allowed to take mommy's jewelry, she looked back at me and said with simple determination, "Mine."

I developed some close friendships with other young families during these early years. We arranged play dates and swapped babysitting to run errands or have some quiet "mommy time." Our neighborhood was full of young families with many children. Backyards were a gathering place for games of ball, riding tricycles and swimming. The park next door was great for basketball, swinging, winter sliding and building snowmen and snow forts. These relationships were vital to our connection with the neighborhood children and other parents. They easily accepted our blended family and Bianca's hyperactivity. Unfortunately, there were other stealing episodes after the bracelet incident.

Bianca and the boys had a special connection with our "Nana," Karl's mom. She lived nearby and was a loving presence in our lives. Nana took each child in turn for special occasions at her home to bake cookies, make grilled cheese sandwiches and have sleepovers. The pre-school years were a happy, busy and easy time for our family. We spent many fun-filled days playing with extended family, neighbors and friends. There were trips to visit relatives and friends as well as regular excursions to local parks and beaches. We rode our bikes and went camping, picnicking and hiking in the woods. It was a sweet time.

When Bianca entered public school kindergarten, I became a room parent and volunteered to chaperone field trips. Karl built a cubby for backpacks, boots and jackets, and we posted a large bulletin board to keep track of homework and school calendar events. We were very organized and worked out the logistics of juggling the schedules of three active school-age children. Each child participated in two activities plus weekly Sunday school, which meant that we were responsible for nine programs overall. During the school years the children were involved with Cub Scouts, Brownie Scouts, synchronized swimming, gymnastics, ballet, soccer, baseball, basketball, karate and music lessons for recorder, piano, trumpet, trombone and flute. Although we were busy, we enjoyed these activities as well as time together at home. Bianca thrived with the simple routines and structure of school, our home and her activities. There were occasional behaviors that surfaced periodically, but we managed each one, chalking them up to normal childhood "bumps in the road" and not giving them much thought or worry.

As a young girl, Bianca was always on the go. She was a flurry of nonstop activity, whether talking, moving or doing. From the time she woke up in the morning until her head touched the pillow at night, she was in constant motion. On her first day of YMCA summer day camp I received a frantic call that she was "lost." A lockdown was in place and the entire staff was combing the grounds for her. The police were notified. A short time later, Bianca was found in the parking lot after much frantic searching. I understood perfectly well how this happened because Bianca moved so fast. I learned from experience to keep her in my sight at all times when in public and to carefully hold her hand, as she had run across a busy street recently without looking. I should have been upset with the YMCA, but I wasn't. I was thankful that she was safe and unharmed, and I was grateful that they were able to locate her so quickly. After that episode, a one-to-one counselor was assigned to watch Bianca for the remainder of summer camp. Fortunately, with this intervention, there were no more incidents at the YMCA. Her impulsivity was a constant danger, however, and I was reminded of this once again later that summer.

We hired an exterminator to treat some pesky carpenter ants and bees and as he entered the driveway, she jumped into his pick-up truck cab. Without hesitation, she stood on the running board and dove headfirst through the open window directly into his lap. I don't know how the poor man managed to keep control of the vehicle, he was so shaken. These examples reinforced my resolve to watch Bianca carefully to prevent "doing before thinking" mishaps.

By the end of first grade it was clear that Bianca was not progressing sufficiently to move into the second grade with her class. She underwent additional educational testing, which resulted in the development of an Individualized Education Plan (IEP) with the school's Special Education Department. The teachers recommended a neuropsychological evaluation in addition to their standardized testing. After receiving pediatrician and insurance approval and pre-authorization, we scheduled an appointment with a pediatric neuropsychologist. After testing was completed, Bianca received a diagnosis of attention deficit hyperactivity disorder (ADHD), auditory processing as well as verbal and receptive language delays. The pediatrician recommended a prescription for Ritalin to help her focus in school and reduce distractibility. We were hesitant to give Bianca a prescription medication and decided to wait. We agreed to give her more time and evaluate the implementation of the IEP to see if repeating grade one would help.

Repeating first grade with the IEP in place did not improve Bianca's learning as the school year unfolded. Even though Bianca's teacher was highly skilled with a certification in Special Education, she was still hyperactive and unable to focus in class. She was struggling even though the curriculum was the same. She was having social difficulties, too. Her impulsivity and hyperactivity resulted in conflict during unstructured time: Arguments, teasing, misunderstandings and tears. Phone calls informing us of Bianca's misdeeds from both the school and concerned parents were common. School and after-school activities were frustrating for everyone. We decided to revisit the neuropsychologist and begin a trial prescription of Ritalin. The "go live" medication date was scheduled and the communication plan between school, teacher, education specialists, school nurse and home was finalized. I gave Bianca the first dose of medication after breakfast, dropped her off at school, went home and held my breath. There were no phone calls. When I picked her up at dismissal time, the teacher reported that after lunch she sat at her desk, put down her pencil and said, "That stupid pill stopped working." We were surprised and delighted that she was able to describe her symptoms so clearly. During school when the medication was working, Bianca was calm, able to participate in class, pay attention and produce legible, correct work. We maintained the daily Ritalin dose for the rest of the school year, and she successfully completed first grade.

Bianca continued to work hard and made progress in second grade with skilled educators and IEP support. The calm routine ended abruptly, however, with another stealing event in December. She took money out of the cafeteria cash register during lunch when staff was distracted. The money was discovered missing, a school-wide search ensued and the money was eventually found in Bianca's backpack. The school scheduled a formal meeting between the principal, guidance counselor, teachers, Special Education specialists and us. In the meantime, she was suspended from school for three days. During the meeting, she did not realize the seriousness of the offense or offer a sincere apology. We were sick with worry. Why did she do this? What did we do wrong? The guilt and shame from having a child steal was overwhelming. The consequence was to ground her in class and not allow her to go outdoors during recess for one month. She was unfazed with the punishment. We agreed that Bianca needed professional help and reached out to our pediatrician to receive authorization and a referral for psychological counseling. In the meantime, she was having trouble fitting in with her Brownie Girl Scout troop because of hyperactivity.

"We can't keep her safe," the scout leader reported. "Bianca runs around during troop meetings and doesn't pay attention. When we went to the city Christmas tree lighting ceremony, she ran across the town common and wouldn't come back to the group when we called her." She was kicked out of

Brownies. Given this and other events, we scheduled our first appointment.

We were able to get an appointment quickly with a child psychologist. Dr. Joanne was experienced, kind and highly qualified. She immediately began work to help Bianca identify her feelings. Bianca did not particularly like going to counseling sessions, but once in the comfort of Dr. Joanne's cozy office, she relaxed and enjoyed the special attention. She began to make progress connecting her feelings with actions. Most of the activities involved play using puppets to safely express thoughts and feelings. At one point during our time together, Dr. Joanne turned and looked directly at me. "I have to ask you some questions that may be hard to hear, but I need you to think carefully and answer honestly," she said. "Does Bianca show remorse after doing something wrong? Does she seem connected to you? Does she care how other people feel? Has she deliberately hurt another being?"

I was startled at the line of questions. I did not think they applied to my daughter, but at the same time I began to have doubts. What if my love for Bianca had blinded me to hidden troubles? Did I ever see these behaviors? Was I ignoring problems? What was wrong with my daughter? I was upset thinking about the intent of these questions. In my heart as her mother, I did not think they applied to Bianca. But a nagging thought wouldn't go away: What if they did apply?

The remainder of second, third and fourth grade passed quickly. There were two trips to the emergency room to disengage a nozzle stuck on her middle finger and set a broken arm, but Bianca otherwise was remarkably healthy and strong. She continued counseling and thrived under Dr. Joanne's care. It was not completely easy during this time. There were occasional parent teacher meetings over inappropriate behavior and she continued to have difficulty during unstructured time such as during gym, recess, lunch room and assembly. Fortunately, the infractions were mild and infrequent and she was doing well. It was a peaceful time. We were occupied with the rhythms of school, homework and after school activities. It was a pleasant mixture of simple routines, family dinners, weekly Sunday school, visiting cousins, scouts, sports, play dates, neighborhood gatherings in our backyard, swimming in the pool and music lessons. We enjoyed summer recreation programs, camping and family vacations. I was busy but able to stay organized and keep up with all of the parenting responsibilities that growing children require. There was much at stake and Bianca was showing significant progress as a result of all our efforts. She was learning to navigate away from home within the safety of the school system, and this supported her normal growth and development during her formative elementary school years.

Bianca's success was because of open communication and coordination between the school and us. We were fortunate to live in a school district that supported her learning needs. She benefited from teacher expertise, additional IEP in-class support plus remedial language and education specialists. The teachers, education specialists, nurse, principal and guidance counselor were partners in our journey through elementary school. We used a daily communication notebook to track Bianca's mood and behavior, identify classroom issues and keep each other informed of homework and struggles at home or in school. We worked together to help her succeed in school and it was working. Her inattention was effectively managed with careful Ritalin dosing and monitoring by her neuropsychologist. Bianca was enrolled in summer school each year between grades to reinforce learning. She enjoyed school and was able to complete each grade successfully. It took a lot of hard work and coordination to schedule and keep up with homework and all of her appointments, meetings and extracurricular activities, but it was worth the effort. I stayed focused and worked with Bianca's team. At the age of 10, all was well with her.

When fifth grade arrived, morning routines, school, recess and free play became more difficult. Bianca could not get out of bed in the morning. This consumed the entire household with daily battles to get to school on time. She screamed at the alarm clock and met the "time to get up!" announcement by burying her head under the pillow and shouting "No!" Once out of bed, what she would wear that day caused further delay. She was often late for school. Garments selected the night before were no longer acceptable. One morning, exhausted, I gave in to avoid a tantrum and allowed her to wear a new pair of party shoes with a half-inch heel. The teachers called during recess to report that she had slipped in her shoes and fallen, chipping her front tooth on the playground cement. Over the next 10 years, this tooth needed multiple root canals, orthodontia work and cosmetic bonding that cost thousands of dollars.

I involved the school office with Bianca's tardiness problem. They suggested that we meet with the principal. He asked, "Bianca, who do you want to wake you up in the morning - your mother or me?" He proceeded. "If you are late for school again, I will personally come over to your house and help you get ready for school." It worked brilliantly. The man was a genius, and I was grateful for his help. After that conversation, morning struggles vanished. She selected clothes the night before. I looked the other way if they "clashed" or didn't match the weather forecast. She quickly learned how to select appropriate clothes after a few instances of being wet, hot or cold because of a wrong outfit choice. She was arriving to school on time and before the morning bell.

As the end of fifth grade approached, emotional outbursts increased both at home and in school. This coincided with the first signs of puberty and hormonal surges. We limped through the remainder of the school year. I tried to keep my head above water, but I was weathering a constant barrage of moodiness, angry outbursts, defiance, swearing, stomping, slamming doors and thrown objects. I was Bianca's target, and I was bewildered. Where did this sudden onset come from? I kept my composure and asserted my parental authority, but the happiness that we once had together was gone. We met with her school team in May to update the IEP and review the test results of a comprehensive education assessment that included a psychological evaluation. The goal was to assess her current learning needs and make a plan for middle school the following year. During the review, Bianca's results were unchanged from previous testing. The psychological evaluation summary, however, was dire. It pointed to a possible increase in anger and defiance. I was cautioned that her transition to middle school and entry into adolescence would be difficult.

The evaluation read, in part, "Bianca chooses actions that at times deliberately provoke others, especially her mother. She has difficulty connecting with her feelings and demonstrates a predisposition for risk-taking and suffers from low self-esteem."

A chill went down my spine. I was afraid of what was in store for her once we left the safety of elementary school.

We enrolled Bianca in the YMCA day camp during the summer between fifth and sixth grade. We continued to bring the children there each summer since the "lost" incident, because of the quality programming, reasonable cost and location. She immediately began to get into trouble. Reports of name calling, taunting and bullying increased as she became more comfortable at camp. Her camp experience ended the day she led a pack of girls to gang up on a camper. They locked the camper in the Port-A-Potty and rocked the stall. Fortunately, the toilet did not tip over but the poor girl was traumatized. Bianca was expelled from camp. The girl's family did not press charges and were satisfied that she was no longer a camper there. The psychological counseling continued. We talked about what happened at camp and why it was bad. We grounded her at home for the remainder of the summer as punishment. This made little impact on her, however, and was more of a punishment for me because she was now constantly at home requiring supervision. I did not get a break. I kept Bianca occupied for the remainder of the summer. We were preparing for a new beginning in middle school in the fall, hoping for success in the new environment but still worried about her behavior and the IEP conclusions.

The first semester of sixth grade passed smoothly with

occasional talking in class and note passing. Bianca was getting to the school bus stop on time, behaving in class, completing homework with her IEP and structured Special Education team. She had one-on-one support in science and social studies and was able to participate in the mainstream classroom. She received separate small group instruction for math and language arts. We met with her guidance counselor, homeroom and Special Education teachers mid-way through the semester. She was on track and making good progress in school. We were thrilled when she made "Principal's List" for her good grades in December. Her school picture was one of the most beautiful a mother could hope for: Neat hair, lovely bright smile and a pretty pink outfit. We were optimistic that middle school would be successful and very happy because it was off to such a good start.

The second semester in sixth grade ushered drama into our household as Bianca became more comfortable in school and simultaneously discovered boys. I was getting regular calls from the guidance counselor and the assistant principal about her behavior. She was fighting with girls. They were heated verbal exchanges, lots of taunting insults and physical fights. There were threats of harm and Bianca was usually the ringleader. Disruptions occurred during unstructured time, on the bus, before and after classes, in the hallway, on the stairwell, during lunch in the cafeteria and gym. She was given several after school detentions and a suspension for the physical fist fight. The school-based police officer was involved because of the level of disruption. She was repeatedly violating the safe school policy. The vice principal was coordinating the discipline. He supported the team recommendations to amend the IEP for more support and supervision during school.

Because of the IEP, we were able to meet with the school regularly and keep apprised of Bianca's progress. Another benefit was that they were trying to help her remain successful in school. As a result, we were able to implement immediate changes as needed. Despite this, I was very worried because she was becoming more volatile and erratic at home. She experienced abrupt mood swings without warning. She was in open defiance against simple requests or house rules. She swore and used vulgar language. Our household was in a constant state of stress and disruption. I was walking on eggshells. Karl was able to help by playing the "good cop" role with her. She related better to him than to me. His presence was vital. He had my back and ran interference to provide moments of much needed peace.

I was extremely careful to use neutral language, exact words and monitor my body language and reactions at all times. I was trying to avoid setting off on an explosive tirade. Every interaction was difficult. She refused simple requests, yelled at me, peppered her language with curse words and called me vile names. She even jumped out at me from hiding, shouting "Ha!" to startle. There was no semblance of civility. If I stated that it was cold, wet or sunny outside — it didn't matter that this was a fact — Bianca would scream that it was not. Communicating with her was impossible. I was trying my best to maintain peace and control for the sake of our family. The boys reacted to the turmoil individually. Michael spent more time out of the house with friends, and Stephen escaped into his artwork. She continued counseling, but it did little to change her behavior. I was doing my best to survive the outbursts. I remained calm, used redirection, limit setting and clear expectations. It was not easy to manage all of this and keep the family running smoothly in the midst of the chaos. I was trying to stay focused and in control. I thought her behavior was due to middle school adjustment, learning disabilities and adolescence. I was hoping that with structure at home and school and a solid IEP in place Bianca would be able to manage her life and get through this difficulty. I was wrong.

chapter 2

THE GATHERING STORM

Our house had a built-in pool with a wrap-around cement deck. On the edge of the deck was a deep fissure occupied by a resident family of garter snakes. Their presence provided countless hours of curiosity for our children and their friends. We were careful to leave them alone, but on occasion one or two would find their way into the bulkhead or nearby bushes, which created panic and coordinated activity to bring them back safely to their home.

One hapless snake left the sanctity of the den and had the misfortune to be captured by Bianca. Considerable time was spent poking at it with sticks. A kitchen knife was added to the experiment, resulting in the inevitable demise. She was excited and hyper-focused on the snake's blood, guts and misery. I was distressed to hear the details. I told her that it upset me to learn that she mistreated another creature. She couldn't let it go. Rather than change the subject, she graphically repeated the events. What she said made me feel sick inside. I was worried as Bianca had never done anything like this before. She had always been empathetic. Now, torture brought satisfaction and she did not show remorse or understand why it was wrong.

Killing the snake unleashed a pattern of behavior without restraint. I was becoming afraid of my daughter, who was now 13. Every look and word from her kept me off balance and nervous. I was constantly waiting for the next explosion. The assault was unrelenting. Normal conversation was impossible. She used foul language and swore at me. "Fucking bitch" replaced "Mom." Every sentence was punctuated with profanity. She stomped her feet and slammed doors. Our house was becoming a war zone, and I was barely able to maintain control. She cut the fabric in a newly purchased dining room chair and carved words into the wooden window sills in the dining room. She wrote on furniture with a permanent marker. She ripped and cut her clothes. Personal hygiene was slipping, also, and she began to smell. She refused to bathe or brush her teeth. Every time I tried to talk and reason with her, she disregarded what I said or ignored me. Worse, she said it never happened and accused me of making things up or exaggerating.

Years later, I learned about "gaslighting," which is a form of mental abuse. The perpetrator twists or spins information, selectively omitting key elements. False information is presented to make a victim doubt their memory, perception or sanity. At the time, I was consumed and trying to keep up with the exhausting drama. I did not have the time or energy to read self-help books or go to a therapist. I was surviving and trying to keep afloat. It took every ounce of strength to continue to work, manage a household, care for our children and maintain a strong marriage.

To say that my husband and I were exhausted is an understatement. Karl was extremely worried about the change in Bianca and did his best to keep steady and maintain his composure through it all. I could not sleep. The assaults were relentless. I suffered from insomnia and startled easily. I analyzed each outburst and my response. Boundaries between normal and abuse blurred. The craziness and turmoil was becoming routine but not normal. It was a cry for help. I was constantly on alert but put up with the abuse because I felt that I had no other choice. I couldn't run away. Our daughter was desperately ill, and I was trying to keep our family together. Sadly, while I was "coping" and trying to maintain the status quo, Bianca was becoming more and more unglued.

Seventh grade started with a bang. We proactively gathered resources: Guidance counselor, Special Education teacher, assistant principal and the school district team chair. An additional behavior plan was added to the IEP. Bianca was attending a small classroom away from the regular school. She was scheduled into two mainstream classes with one-on-one staff support. Instruction in a quiet, contained environment helped her focus. Immersion in a regular classroom provided academic support, prevented inappropriate behavior and helped her engage with peers. There was also a quiet space away from the hustle of middle school complete with soft lighting, couches and additional staff. She could access this respite when feeling overwhelmed or if she needed a safe place to cool off. The team was on alert to intervene when Bianca's behavior began to escalate. School bus transportation was changed because the regular bus was too unstructured, and the bus driver could not control her. Bianca was picked up at the end of our driveway in a small van monitored by a staff member in addition to the driver. We held our collective breaths as the new plan got underway and September progressed into October.

It did not last. We began to see more disturbing signs. Bianca was unable to hear the word "no." Limit setting was met with fierce resistance, wild tantrums, verbal assaults, increased swearing and threats. Once again, we were walking on eggshells all the time, waiting for the next explosion. She was behaving similarly in school and received many detentions for disruptive behavior in class, in hallways, the cafeteria and before and after school. She was also getting into fights with other girls. At home, it was becoming impossible to complete homework or get her out the door on time for school pick-up. Bianca would not go to bed on time and was up most of the night walking around the house snacking and watching TV. My sleep was constantly interrupted. Each time I heard noise or smelled food cooking, I got up. This usually led to a verbal exchange.

"Bianca, it's late and time to go to bed," I would say. "Please put away the food and turn off the light." "Fuck you!" she would reply. "You can't make me."

The marks on the inside of her forearm started out as

superficial skin rubbings made with the metal edge of a pencil eraser. She began hanging around with a group of middle school girls who were known "cutters." I accidently came across a picture of a classmate with deep cuts on her arms on Bianca's phone. The girl was smiling and holding her bleeding arms toward the camera. I had never heard of cutting before but realized that what I was seeing was serious. I called the school and reported what I had found. What began innocently quickly progressed and became a regular way for Bianca to cope. She transitioned from rubbing her skin raw to cutting. The self-inflicted lacerations became deeper and more frequent. She cut herself with pointy metal edges: Unfurled paper clips, staples, spiral notebook wires and pierced earring studs. I locked up all of our household knives to limit access and increased the frequency of counseling sessions. I didn't know what else to do. I was reassured that the cuts, although disturbing, provided an emotional release. They worked as a safety valve to get rid of unexpressed, pent-up feelings. The cuts were superficial and thankfully did not get infected. I followed the counselor's recommendation and did not pay a lot of attention to this behavior. I tried to treat it in a matter-of-fact way. The theory was that if I focused on her cutting, this would reinforce the behavior and make it worse. To see my child cut her beautiful skin and try to remain calm was excruciating. The strategy did not work and the cutting got much worse. Within a few weeks, the school called to report that Bianca threatened to kill a classmate and had cut herself in front of other children. They called the police and she was expelled from school.

I took time off from work and went to Juvenile Court in our county to file a Child In Need of Services (CHINS) petition.

I completed the paperwork, providing details of Bianca's recent events to the court clerk. I cited the cutting episodes, verbal and physical incidents, behaviors at home, all of the school problems and my concerns. I kept notes of everything and brought them with me. I had personal memos to memory of things said and done, details of every appointment and counseling session, dates and outcomes of school meetings, a copy of Bianca's latest IEP and each amendment. I printed e-mails, notices of school detentions and suspensions. I even brought my home-to-school communication log. This meticulous documentation strengthened the affidavit and supported the fact that we needed help. Our family was in trouble and Bianca was out of control. We had done everything to get the support of her counselor and school but it was not enough. Filing a CHINS was one of the best things I did. I used the authority of the court system to help her and get help. I was impressed with the professionalism of the court staff. They took my report seriously. It was so sad to be there but I felt hopeful. It was even sadder to see the faces of other parents in Juvenile Court that morning. The corridors and benches were crowded with a wide assortment of parents, social workers, attorneys and children. Everyone looked stressed and unhappy. Even in this crowd with other parents facing similar issues, I felt alone.

A court hearing date was set and I left with the CHINS copy in hand. I felt as if I was making progress and had the weight of the court to back my parental authority. The rules were listed on a piece of paper: Follow parent requests and house rules, go to school on time, stay out of trouble and go to all counseling appointments. The court took Bianca's behavior seriously and dealt with our situation in a no-

nonsense manner. She signed the form, complied with the CHINS rule, served her school suspension and returned to classes. She did not miss any appointments and generally behaved herself. It was a welcome respite. On the appointed court date, Bianca appeared before the judge, humble and diminutive with all evidence of past aggression gone. She was nervous and scared and agreed to the rules set by the judge. She was appointed a probation officer to enforce expectations. The probation officer would check on Bianca during school and randomly at home in the evening. If she violated the court order she would return before the judge and could be sent to juvenile detention, commonly known as "juvy" in street talk.

But soon, the explosive behavior, verbal outbursts and physical aggression began to increase at home and in school in spite of the CHINS court order. I attended regular meetings at school because of continuing problems. There were many e-mails and phone calls between the school team, counselor, probation officer and me. Church was becoming impossible to get through. Bianca would put her feet on the pew in front of us, throw the hymnals, spit on the floor and swear. Her actions reminded me of scenes from "The Exorcist." It was as if she were possessed. Things were worse at home. She would sneak up behind me and jump out shouting, "Ha!" She was trying to startle and scare me, and it worked. I was on constant guard and felt as if I was going to be attacked at any minute. At other times, she glared at me and would refuse to speak. When she did speak, she told me that she hated me, that I wasn't her "real" mother and that she wished I were dead. I was unable to make a request or ask her a simple question. She would respond with "I hate you," "You can't make me" or simply, "Fuck you!" Our home continued to be a war zone. She had a complete disregard for house rules and my authority. Bianca was spiraling downward, and I was afraid that she was taking me with her.

Everything came to a head one evening when Karl had taken the boys to a scouting event in Boston, and she and I were alone in the house. The day had been tense and stressful. Bianca was on the computer and it was well past her bedtime. I began with a 15-minute bedtime reminder and repeated it again at the five-minute mark. She ignored me. I repeated that it was time to turn off the computer and get ready for bed, but once again I was ignored. I then proceeded to say that if she did not log off the computer and get ready for bed right then, I would unplug the modem. She exploded, slammed the computer mouse down, stomped past me and deliberately pushed me aside — hard. I looked at her and said, "What was that about?" She stopped in front of me, looked directly into my eyes and said clearly without any emotion in her voice, "Next time, I will hurt myself and tell them that you did it!" I was horrified because I knew that she was capable of carrying through with her threat and I was helpless to stop her. Although I had been afraid of her before, for the first time I was afraid for me.

Bianca did eventually go to her room but refused to take a shower or get ready for bed. I went out on the deck to get some fresh air and clear my thoughts. We had entered dangerous territory. I wasn't sure what to do, but I knew that this could not continue. When Karl came home, we talked and made a plan. The next morning after I got her on the school bus, at the urging of my husband I placed a call to my primary care doctor. I was a nervous wreck, had a splitting headache, nausea and dizziness. In the examination room, my blood pressure was dangerously high. The nurse practitioner spent a long time getting the history and details of my situation. I remember her words. "This is not normal and you do not have to live like this," she said. "You are in danger and you need to get your daughter help right now. I am giving you a medical letter to be excused from work today. You need to take care of this situation and yourself immediately."

After leaving my doctor's office, I called to notify work of my absence and began the next steps.

Karl and I had agreed that we had to get Bianca help, but we were not sure exactly know how to do this. I made calls to her team to get advice. I spoke with her counselor to tell her about the conversation the previous evening. She agreed that Bianca was in full-blown crisis and needed an immediate psychological evaluation in the emergency room. She instructed me to call Bianca's pediatrician and give details of what was happening. She called our pediatrician and the school counselor, as well, and I also called the school guidance counselor. The pediatrician made arrangements for her to be screened in the emergency room and the counselor gave them a report. I picked her up from school, and we drove to the hospital. This was a bad decision. Bianca was furious. She swore and glared at me for the entire trip. I had engaged the child locks on the car door so she could not jump out. The hospital was less than a mile away, but it was a long and stressful trip.

The emergency room staff was waiting for us, and they were

extremely professional and kind. I completed admission forms and answered their questions such as "What happened? Why are you concerned? What did she say and what did she do?" Karl arrived shortly after. We waited in the lobby before we could join Bianca in the locked psychiatric wing of the emergency room. A security guard was posted outside of her room. All of her clothing and possessions were removed. I helped her get into a hospital gown, and the physician arrived within a few minutes to perform a complete history and physical examination. The nurse returned, re-took her vital signs and administered anti-anxiety medication. Bianca was strangely calm and cooperative. It was as if the security provided by the emergency room made her feel safe. A social worker completed an intake assessment. She contacted the school and Bianca's counselor to get their perspective. The decision was then made to commit her to a psychiatric hospital. We were cautioned that we could be waiting a long time in the emergency room because of a shortage of available pediatric beds. We agreed with the recommendation. Bianca was "pink slipped" because she was a danger to herself and others. She could not leave the hospital and we would not take her home.

There are no words to describe the helplessness and terror of committing your child to a psychiatric hospital. I pray that no parent ever has to experience this. But in my heart, I knew it was the only logical choice because Bianca was so sick and out of control. I was overwhelmed and sad that we had come to this point, yet in a strange way I was relieved. Karl and I had traveled an exhausting journey these past few years and wore ourselves out trying to stabilize our daughter. While I was reassured that she was getting the help she desperately needed, I also felt guilty that we couldn't handle her at home any longer.

We waited the remainder of the afternoon and into the evening. Six hours later we received good news. There was a pediatric psychiatric bed available nearby. When the ambulance arrived to transport Bianca, I signed the necessary paperwork then went home to pack a few essential items for her stay: A change of clothes, pajamas, toiletries, flip-flops and her favorite blanket and pillow. I reassured the boys that their sister was safe and was going to get help. They understood that she was in a hospital for children with emotional problems and were relieved. I realized then how much Bianca's instability had affected our family and the burden they also carried. I kissed both goodnight and drove to the hospital. I parked the car and followed directions (immediate family only) to the locked pediatric psychiatric unit. It seemed surreal to be looking for a hospital entrance to join our daughter in a psychiatric hospital.

The elevator closed behind me and I was buzzed into a foyer. I was asked if I had any weapons or sharp objects or a cell phone. My cell phone and pocketbook were placed in a locker. Bianca's overnight bag was taken into the nurse station and searched for dangerous objects or contraband - anything that could be used as a weapon or to self- injure. The orderly escorted me into the conference room and instructed me to wait for the nurse to begin the admission process. I looked around. Everything was quiet and contained. The space was antiseptic and bare. Patients' artwork, posters and inspirational messages hung on the walls. The effect fell short of its intention. The result was depressing and sad.

In a few moments Bianca came in; she looked small and scared. The aggressive posturing of the previous day was gone. She gave me a big hug and asked, "When can I go home, Mommy?" Her voice trembled, "I want to go home. I want to see my brothers. Please?"

It was a heartbreaking, sincere plea but impossible to allow. The admission nurse entered the room, and I completed the paperwork granting permission to commit our daughter. When it was all over, I kissed Bianca goodbye and left the building. I sat in my car for a very long time looking up at the night sky before I was able to drive home. It had been a grueling day, and I was spent. But I was also relieved that Bianca was safe and getting the care she desperately needed. At the same time, I was overwhelmed and so very sad. I desperately needed sleep. Our family was getting a much deserved break from the intensity of recent months, and I was looking forward to having peace and time to spend with the boys without all the drama. Bianca was exactly where she needed to be as hard as this was for all of us.

Bianca remained in the hospital for 10 days and missed Thanksgiving. It was the first holiday we had been separated. I cried a lot but put on a brave front. It was heartbreaking to go through the motions of holiday preparations while our daughter was committed to a psychiatric hospital. Attending the holiday parade and watching the carefree celebrations of families was awful. Our daughter should have been celebrating with us. The smiling faces of happy teens marching in the band and color guard were a stark contrast to what Bianca was experiencing. It was a lonely, sad place to be. Our family was not the same as other families. We were living with mental illness, and there was no race for the cure or rally for this awful disease. I hoped that Bianca could get well and rejoin life. I couldn't fix this on my own.

Bianca's commitment had a hidden benefit. Our home life was quiet again. We were able to enjoy peaceful meals together. The tension was gone. The boys were more carefree than they had been in a long time. I caught up on much needed sleep while enjoying the respite. I was able to relax and life drifted back to normal. But, once again, it would not last. As preparations were made for Bianca's discharge, my anxiety began to increase.

After 10 days in the hospital, her discharge plan was finalized; she was coming home. I was given a handful of prescriptions for a 30-day supply of her anti-depressant and mood stabilizer medications. I was also given a list of psychiatrists to contact. I had to find a provider and make an appointment so that Bianca's medications would continue beyond the 30-day supply. The hospital gave me a list of emergency telephone numbers, as well. We were buzzed out the door. It was much easier to leave than to be admitted. Our support was gone. We were on our own. I was responsible for arranging Bianca's ongoing mental health care. The hospital had met its obligation to contain and stabilize her. They did not offer follow-up care, additional treatment, psychiatric help or coordination of services. It was all up to us.

I immediately began to make telephone calls from the list. I tried to remain calm and keep a positive outlook. We had excellent health insurance and, as a nurse, I knew how to connect with health care services. My optimism quickly dimmed, however. Most providers did not accept insurance; we would have to pay their fee directly and collect reimbursement from our insurer. This might be difficult because our claim would likely be rejected if we chose a psychiatrist "out of network" as our primary care physician would not approve pre-authorization. I was learning the language of insurance the hard way. Other psychiatrists were not accepting new patients. Some practices with availability were over an hour's drive away, and appointment times interfered with Bianca's school day or our work schedules. Her medication supply was dwindling with each passing day and I was starting to panic. I did eventually find a local pediatric psychiatrist who accepted our insurance and was admitting new patients. I was relieved and made an appointment for the next available opening.

We walked into the psychiatrist's office and I was immediately overwhelmed. The office was filled with clocks: Cuckoo, pendant, alarm, analog, digital, plastic, antique, grandfather, ship clocks and more. They were precisely timed to chime, ding, dong, chirp, bell, buzz, whistle and alarm in precise synchrony at the hour. It was unnerving and a little weird, I thought. In spite of this quirk, the physician was affable and extremely professional, and I liked him immediately. He was capable and very kind. He reviewed the copies of Bianca's discharge paperwork and medical records that we brought and asked a lot of questions. Bianca was prescribed the necessary medication, and we scheduled a follow-up appointment. Bianca was disengaged during most of the visit. She answered his questions with monosyllabic, sarcastic responses. While I was mortified at her rude behavior, the doctor was unperturbed. He scribbled notes after each response and nodded his head in a grandfatherly, understanding manner. At least she wasn't putting on a pretense, I thought. Her attitude perfectly reflected the way she really was. We left his office much relieved. I felt fortunate to have found him and very optimistic that Bianca was going to be stabilized now that she was properly overseen with a psychiatrist managing her condition and medications.

I was busy bringing Bianca to the lab to monitor medication levels and continuing communication with the education team at school and her counselor. She was making gains during weekly counseling sessions, identifying triggers that made her angry and learning how to control outbursts. I continued to keep a journal of daily events, observations, appointments, professional contact information and discussions. I was worried that Bianca could regress at any time but hopeful that with the right supports in place now, she would remain stable and continue to improve.

Bianca's anger and defiance did eventually begin to surface. As before, I became the target of her abuse. She refused to eat at regular mealtime and snacked throughout the day. Bathing and hygiene were minimal. She was up late at night and unable to get out of bed in the morning for school. Her bedroom was a mess. There were dirty dishes, plates of leftover food in her bed and half-empty drinks on the floor. She left wet towels on furniture. Clothes were strewn about the house. Lights were left on, doors left open. Spills remained untouched where they fell. When she did bathe, sans soap, the bathroom looked like a walrus had been in the tub. Puddles of water, gobs of shampoo, hair gel, toothpaste and body wash were left behind in prodigious amounts. The house was in chaos, and family meals became battlefields. She refused to pick up after herself, and it was easier to avoid the battle and do it myself. Every word triggered an argument. Cell phone use was another fight. I blocked inappropriate materials and limited user times, but it was impossible to completely manage. She fell asleep while streaming songs at night, and this careless mishap added $2,000 in charges to one monthly bill. We were caught in the vicious up-down cycle of mental illness once again.

I was sitting at my desk at work when I received a call to come immediately to school. Bianca had threatened to kill another child and, when confronted, she threatened to kill herself. The police and ambulance were at the school on standby. I walked to my car with a pit in my stomach. The skies were gray and raining cold icy drops, which matched my mood pretty well. I placed an emergency call to Karl, Bianca's psychiatrist, counselor and pediatrician. This time the plan was familiar; the team sprang into action. Bianca would go directly to the hospital for an emergency psychiatric screening. Unfortunately, we had done this before. What was going to be new this time, I wondered? We were familiar with the drill and thought that another hospitalization would help to stabilize her, perhaps with a medication adjustment or other treatment.

I was buzzed into the school and escorted to the main office. Bianca was sitting in the lobby with her guidance counselor as I sat down beside them. She was fuming. Parents, students and office staff hurried about their business in hushed tones with furtive glances toward us. The vice principal came out of his office and was very firm. Bianca's behavior was unacceptable, and she was immediately suspended from school. She could not return. There would be a team meeting to determine her school placement after she was cleared by her psychiatrist. I understood his responsibility to keep the school safe and maintain discipline but thought the conversation should have been held privately. I was sad and humiliated for my daughter. Bianca was in crisis and needed help. Public school was not a good environment for her, and it was no one's fault. We had all tried to make it work, using every available resource in the school and at home. I gave the educators a lot of credit for their efforts on our behalf. It clearly was not working anymore. Bianca needed a different plan. We left middle school and never returned.

The emergency room was waiting for us and we were immediately escorted into the locked psychiatric area. I recognized the same guard as before stationed outside her door. There was no turning back. The psychiatric screening process was hauntingly familiar. The staff was professional and wrote down everything we said. I had with me copies of Bianca's IEP, school communication, attendance list and her most recent report card. I also brought my notebook containing observations, school communications and notes to memory. All of these documents gave an accurate picture of Bianca and were helpful to the emergency room staff.

One of the best habits I developed over the years was to keep notes. They weren't fancy. I wrote names, appointment dates, addresses and telephone numbers of all Bianca's providers. The notes also contained my follow-up meeting "to do" lists as well as team communications. I kept a diary of daily observations and the notebook was full. I kept it up to date and carried it with me at all times. I was thankful I had these papers with me in the emergency room. My habit of carrying this information was vital in times of crisis because I could not always rely on my memory.

Bianca looked small on the examination table with her knees

tucked under her chin. We were in the psychiatric room once again. There were no mirrors, door knobs, hooks or faucet handles. The room had been carefully sanitized so there was no way for her to hurt herself or anyone else. She was under continuous camera surveillance. After a few minutes the physician, nurse and crisis counselor completed their assessments in turn. They asked her if she wanted to hurt herself or anyone else. She was honest and said that yes, sometimes she did. They examined her physically and took note of her hygiene and the multiple cuts in various stages of healing on her arms. The counselor read my notes and talked to Bianca's psychiatrist, counselor and the school guidance counselor. The decision was made to admit Bianca to a pediatric psychiatric hospital once more. We agreed with the plan and were cautioned that it might take some time to find a space for her. Even though I was familiar with the process and knew about limited bed availability, it was still awful to experience this psychiatric admission again. I was sick with worry about Bianca's mental health and her future. At the same time, it was comforting to know that Bianca was getting more help.

Within a few hours a bed was located. Unfortunately, it was farther away than the previous hospital - one hour by car. The previous hospital was located in the next town, a 10-minute drive from our house. When the ambulance came to pick up Bianca, I signed the papers and went home to pack a bag of essential toiletries and clothes. I was able to catch my breath, have a cup of tea and a slice of toast. The night was cold and dark and the decision was made that I would remain home and Karl would go to the hospital, given the late hour and distance.

The next morning, I took a personal day off from work, and we drove 60 miles to the hospital. Whereas the first hospital was cheerful and bright, this one by contrast was dark and was housed in a building that reminded me of a World War II bunker. Bianca was curled under her covers asleep in her room and it was almost noon. She was disheveled and had wet the bed. She was more withdrawn than we had ever seen her before and looked drugged. I helped her get showered and dressed. We packed the soiled clothes to launder at home and sat together for a while in the community lounge.

The patients here were older than those in the previous hospital. There were no school-age children, only adolescents in the throes of crisis. Most sported a variety of vicious tattoos, wild clothing and hair. They looked street savvy and dangerous. Our daughter was one of the youngest patients there. We were helpless to shelter her from the raw reality of full-blown adolescent mental illness. It was on full display here, and I was worried that she would be negatively influenced by it. During the course of this hospitalization, she formed friendships with some of these patients. Much to my dismay, they exchanged telephone numbers and details of their journey to this place. I was helpless to intervene and worried about these connections. While I was grateful for the psychiatric care Bianca was receiving, I was also afraid for her. The hospital space was not conducive to healing. There were weak fluorescent light fixtures hanging from the ceiling. The light cast a yellow hue to everything it touched. The cement walls were coated in a thick coat of industrial-strength yellow paint. The combined effect of paint and lighting was to render everything the color of urine. The furniture fared no better. It sported rough plaid fabric that was torn and stained in many places. It was noisy, loud and disorganized. Patients wandered around aimlessly but perked up when visitors arrived. We were solicited for spare change and cigarettes. Days were long with minimal structured time. There was nothing for Bianca to do except watch television in the communal lounge, eat or remain in her room. When we visited, the staff looked bored and disinterested. During her hospitalization, the psychiatrist prescribed two additional medications to help balance her mood. There was twice daily group therapy sessions that patients were encouraged to attend. As far as I could tell, Bianca participated in this activity but otherwise there was minimal individualized therapy. It seemed as if Bianca was simply occupying a bed until her release. I had my doubts about the effectiveness of this hospitalization and wasn't sure if she was better off here after all.

After discharge, we convened an emergency meeting with Bianca's school team, counselor and the director of Special Education. There was unanimous agreement that the traditional public school setting was not a good fit for Bianca. She would require a separate, behavioral-based school. As luck would have it, there was one in our community and it had an opening. The school was organized, efficient, well managed and had an excellent reputation. The teachers and counselors were highly skilled in managing adolescent behaviors. The enrollment process would take several weeks to complete, and Bianca would remain suspended while the admission paperwork was finalized. In the meantime, she continued weekly sessions with her counselor and met with her psychiatrist to receive prescriptions for the new medications. The hospital arranged for Bianca to attend an outpatient day program while we were waiting for admission to the new school. This was a transition program for adolescents at least 14 years old. The goal was to bridge in-patient psychiatric hospitalization with a structured program to support community re-entry post discharge. This program was perfect for Bianca because it did exactly what it set out to accomplish: Provide a smooth bridge between hospital and home. If I could have predicted the bizarre turn of events from being in this program, however, I would have made other arrangements.

I received a telephone call from the outpatient counselor. He wanted me to come to the school one hour prior to Bianca's dismissal to meet with him. I was surprised and curious about the purpose of this meeting but left work early to comply with the request. When I arrived, the counselor inquired how Bianca was punished at home. After I explained our parenting style, he informed me of an event that Bianca shared during group meeting. When asked if she was ever hit by someone, Bianca told her team that we hit our children regularly. As a result of this accusation, the program was required by law to report us to the Department of Social Services (DSS) for investigation into the allegation of child abuse and assault and battery.

This began a three-month long inquisition nightmare. We were treated like criminals and it felt like a witch trial. In this court of law we were guilty until proven innocent. The finger pointing triggered an automatic agency response. There was no room for professional judgment or discernment as to the validity of the charge. In fairness, the social workers were just doing their job, fulfilling the requirements the child abuse law demanded. I remembered Bianca's previous threat to falsely accuse me of assault. I cried at the injustice of the process and was sick with worry that the investigators would believe Bianca's lie. I was afraid that my professional nursing license could be in jeopardy. I had no recourse. All I could do was wait helplessly while the system determined my guilt or innocence. The DSS Social Workers interviewed us and our children separately. We provided names of family and friends who could vouch for our integrity and parenting ability. We were engaged in an all out campaign to clear the charge and prevent damage to our personal and professional reputations. It was unbelievable that we had to go through this ordeal. We had been subjected to Bianca's abuse, violence and threats for years. Now we were the accused. The irony of the situation would have been laughable except that it was very real and scary. Bianca did not care that we were traumatized. She did not show any concern that we were upset and had to go through the ordeal of her making. In fact, she looked like she was rather enjoying the show.

I will be forever grateful to our dear friends and family who stood by our side during this trial. They challenged DSS with questions such as "Why wasn't Bianca's reliability as a witness questioned, given her history?" They eloquently gave examples and described our ability to effectively parent under extreme conditions. We would not have gotten through the investigation without their unwavering support.

Well intended legislation meant to protect vulnerable children from harm requires reporting. I understand that. Caution, however, must be taken in situations where mentally ill children accuse their parents of abuse. It is a serious charge. We were put into the same category as convicted child abusers and treated like criminals. I lost a lot of sleep and was upset at the unfairness of it all.

The charges were eventually dropped due to a lack of evidence. There was no apology from DSS or the outpatient program. We were free from the ordeal, but the damage was done. I made a vow to never be put in that position again. If attacked, I would not fight back. The risk to my professional reputation, personal integrity and marriage was too high.

My heart breaks for abused children. We never abused ours. Quite the opposite, we were under a continuous barrage of emotional abuse, verbal attacks and physical threats from Bianca. It was hurled at us constantly, day in and day out, driven by the demon of mental illness. It was as if the gates of Hell had opened. I held my ground through every assault. I refused to lower myself to her level and react in anger. But I was not going to lie down like a doormat and be a victim, either. I vowed to survive even though I had been deeply wounded. Unfortunately, this ordeal created another chasm in my relationship with Bianca from which I never fully recovered.

Bianca continued to cut herself regularly. I cleansed and bandaged each laceration. Because of my ministrations, they did not get infected or require suturing. It was nonetheless heartbreaking and distressing to see her beautiful skin so scarred. More disturbing was that she began to see and hear hallucinations.

"When I look in the mirror I see someone else," she said. "It is a blonde girl most of the time, but sometimes there are other faces that scare me. I'm afraid of what they will say to me. I hear their voices." Bianca's medication was adjusted and the frequency of counseling sessions was increased. The counselor suggested covering her bedroom mirror as this was where the visions were seen. We covered the dresser mirror with purple silk fabric which, with the medication, did work to stop the hallucinations. We decided that it was also a good time to freshen up her bedroom and change the décor. The walls were painted pale lavender and the bookshelf soft pink. Bianca and I silk-screened her sheer curtains, and we put a floral wallpaper border on the wall. A pretty bedspread and throw pillows pulled the room together beautifully. The effect was tranquil and vintage girl teen and, most importantly, Bianca loved it.

Bianca was missing on the school bus to go home one afternoon after April school vacation. I received an emergency call from the school and phoned Bianca on her cell phone. She answered and was home with a friend. They were watching television with her brothers. I breathed a sigh of relief but was angry that she deliberately broke a house rule. As a working mother, all after school plans were made in advance between the school and parents. Bianca got a ride from a mother by lying and telling her that I was home. The unwitting mother took her at her word and dropped the children off without verification. This was the first time she lied to another adult and manipulated a situation to get her way. A few weeks later, the school called again to report that Bianca walked out of school, threatening to run away. The police were searching for her. I was on my way to the school when I received welcome news. Bianca was found. She was walking on a street and did not run away when the police approached. Instead, she sat on the curb but refused to get into the cruiser. The officers were patient and able to talk with her. She eventually calmed down enough to agree to go to the hospital. I arrived at the scene as the ambulance was leaving and, after speaking with the police, followed it to the emergency room.

Bianca was admitted to a psychiatric hospital for the third time. Unfortunately, I was familiar with the process, by now our third emergency room visit, although it was still stressful and sad for all of us. This incident was triggered with behavioral limit setting in the school. Bianca was angry that she was expected to follow rules and she bolted. We were lucky she was found but realized that continued cutting, hallucinations, lying to adults and running away were big safety concerns. Bianca remained hospitalized for several days while her medications were adjusted. She was discharged with all supports in place: Counselor, prescriber and school. There was nothing else to do but continue with the school placement, counseling, psychiatric appointments and medication treatment. We were still worried but kept hoping she would get better.

On the way to a counseling appointment Bianca got angry. It might have been because she didn't want to go, or it could have been because of something I said. An offhand comment, a look she didn't like — the triggers were a hidden landmine. Usually, I could avoid setting her off. I learned what to say, how to say it and, most importantly, what not to say. When I did speak, my word selection and tone of voice were chosen carefully. It was hard and I did not always do well. This time, whatever the trigger, the results were explosive. She swore, screamed at me and threatened to jump out of the car. The ride from our house to the counselor took less than five minutes, but I was trapped. I could not stop or pull over because I was afraid that she would bolt. My eyes were fixed on the road. I could not turn back and had to get us to the appointment safely. By the time we arrived, I was shaking and Bianca was still at full throttle. The staff took one look at us and immediately assessed the situation. Bianca's counselor escorted her into a safe room and the psychiatrist called 911 to arrange for an ambulance to bring Bianca to the emergency room.

The hospital emergency room psychiatric screening was routine although still exhausting and stressful, but at least now we knew what to expect. Bianca was hospitalized again and during this hospitalization we were encouraged to apply for Department of Mental Health (DMH) services. This process, although lengthy, would expand psychiatric services and the availability of in-patient beds if she were a client on their caseload. We completed the necessary paperwork, got copies of medical records, in-patient psychiatric admission and discharge notes, counselor notes, school notes, IEPs and insurance forms. We were cautioned that the first application was usually denied. We painstakingly completed all the required documents, signatures and statements.

Within a few weeks we had an appointment with a DMH intake referral specialist. We met to review the application whereupon a formal "determination of need" assessment was completed. The meeting proceeded smoothly. Shortly thereafter Bianca was accepted onto their caseload, given the meticulous documentation and her extensive history. We were relieved and grateful. As a DMH client, Bianca qualified to receive extra support and resources.

Bianca was on a lot of medication: Anti-depressants, mood stabilizers and anti-psychotics. She was diagnosed with bipolar disorder, attention deficit hyperactivity disorder, suicide ideation, reactive attachment disorder and schizoaffective disorder. Her affect was flat and she looked drugged. The wild behavior was under control but her spark was gone. Something was not right with this treatment plan. The side effects were significant, and although her blood levels were within normal limits the psychiatrist decided to adjust her medication regimen. The goal was to prescribe the least amount of medication while achieving the best effect. Over the next few months the medications were adjusted. Slowly and carefully the meds were dialed back, and we began to see our daughter's personality re-emerge.

The cycle of medication, counselor appointments, psychiatrist meetings and school continued. A bright spot during this time was Bianca's involvement in the girls' synchronized swim team at our local YMCA. Bianca practiced three days a week and spent a total of 12 hours in the water with her team. It was a rigorous workout with skilled, kind coaches and a lot of fun. Bianca enjoyed the grace and beauty of this activity. She was incredibly strong in the water and had a great time pushing herself to the limit. During one fundraiser, the girls asked for pledges for each lap they swam. One lap equaled down and back without stopping in the Olympic-size pool. It was for a good cause so I pledged $1 per lap. Bianca swam 83 laps without stopping. She came out of the pool for a quick drink of water and then went back in to swim 34 more laps. I couldn't believe it! Bianca's stamina and swim style were incredible. The coaches were quite impressed. I happily wrote a check for $117. But soon after this event, the swim coach told me that Bianca was difficult to manage in the water, on deck and in the locker room. She wasn't listening to the coaches and was swearing at them. Mothers were complaining, also. She taunted her teammates and swore at them. Mothers who previously had been friendly began to avoid us. The final straw happened in the locker room. Bianca showed the girls how she cut her arms. She was asked to leave the team. We had no choice. Bianca could not stay and cause such havoc. I said goodbye to the coaches. Bianca did not express sadness or remorse at any of this. "Good. I hate synchro," she said. She did not say goodbye to anyone.

School was difficult and once again Bianca was out of control in the classroom, screaming and swearing and running out of the building with staff chasing her to return. On several occasions this required police intervention. Each event resulted in a school suspension. Her behavior at home was just as bad. She slammed doors, swore, cut herself and refused to follow family norms, rules or routines. The familiar cycle of increasing aggression, threats of self-harm and school suspensions led to a fourth hospitalization in late winter. This time, with DMH support an in-patient bed was located quickly. I was beside myself with exhaustion and fear and I was at the end of my rope. The family was suffering. The boys were beginning to have difficulty in school. Our home was a war zone once more. It was decided that even with everything in place at home, in school and in the community Bianca could not continue on this path. She was admitted to a psychiatric hospital again. This time was different. It was agreed that she would not be coming home to live with us after discharge.

chapter **3**

CONTAINMENT

Bianca was discharged from the hospital directly to the Highlander House, a group home for adolescents. It was managed by the DMH, and she qualified for a bed there because she was on their caseload and the hospital said she was not ready to come home.

Bianca could not have cared less. She was not worried about going to a strange place. Dressed in jeans and a T-shirt, she listened to her music through headphones.

The house was at the end of a long residential neighborhood in a small town on the Merrimack River. As we pulled into the driveway, I was struck by how normal it looked. The parking lot next to the garage was the only indication that the house served another purpose. When we arrived, we waited in the vestibule just inside the front door. The house was sprawling and lay out in the shape of an L. It had a large, sunny family room with lots of casual couches and a wall of books and games. There was a large bulletin board with various memos, schedules and posted house rules tacked to it. In a few moments we were greeted by Laura, the weekend house supervisor. Dressed in a plaid shirt and chinos, she had a sweet lilting voice, freckles and long brunette hair pulled back into a loose bun. She looked more like a college student than the administrator of a group home. I was immediately put at ease with her bubbly kindness.

We were led to Bianca's room. The room was in the girls' corridor directly off the main entrance. There were four rooms, each equipped with four bunk beds and a large bathroom at the end of the corridor. Her room was fitted with two bunk beds and four bureaus. I helped her unpack and we made her bunk on the lower berth complete with floral sheets, pillows and comforter. Once finished we completed the intake process, signed papers listing emergency contact information and permission to treat. We also made an appointment to return on the following business day to meet with the program director and Bianca's counselor. The house was quiet, as the clients were out on a shopping trip with the rest of the staff. The environment was clean and well maintained. The team would coordinate communication with her private counselor and DMH case manager, as well as with the public school. There was a nurse and psychiatrist on staff, as well. For now, I did not have to manage medication or any of Bianca's appointments.

When we said our goodbyes, I was not sad that Bianca was not coming home with me. I was relieved and hopeful that this treatment program would help her. I felt as if a great weight had been lifted. She was getting help, and our family was getting a much needed break. We were expected to attend weekly family counseling sessions and were encouraged to visit regularly, which we did.

It was clear that despite all of the resources put in place to stabilize and keep Bianca at home and in school, it was not enough. Everything we tried had failed. It was necessary for her to be in a secure environment where professionals could manage and contain the violence and self-destruction. It was the only way she was going to get well. The Highlander House contracted with our hometown to authorize out of district school placement. Our public school paid the education costs for Bianca's schooling at Highlander, and the DMH paid for the psychiatric residential care. It felt strange for her to be living somewhere else, but I was encouraged with the plan and relieved that I didn't have to manage her care any longer.

Bianca began to make progress. She took her medication, kept herself and her personal space clean and she followed house rules. She cooked, cleaned and participated in group activities. Our visits were pleasant and calm. She was genuinely glad to see us, and although we were not allowed to take her off property we enjoyed our time together chatting, walking outside or, on occasion, playing board games. I brought her special items from home: Art supplies, note cards, pictures, toiletries and hair accessories. She settled into the daily routine with ease. It was a good place for her and she seemed happy.

Although Bianca was stable and making progress at Highlander, within a short time, it was decided that she needed longer treatment. The team felt that her mental illness was too severe for their program. Plans were made to transition her into a long-term residential facility called Solace. I was surprised at this turn of events although Bianca took the news well. We soon said goodbye to the Highlander team, packed her belongings in the car and drove to the new group home. This would be her new home until she was safe to come home.

It was a relief to be free of the constant stress of living with a child who had a major psychiatric illness. We had been thrust into the world of self-destruction and violence. We exhausted every possibility to help her and in the process had exhausted ourselves. Our family was strained, almost to the breaking point. Nothing had worked, including medication, counseling, day treatment, special public schools or the juvenile court. We had been consumed with the cycles of escalation, threats, violence, self-destruction and hospitalization. I lost count of the number of professionals we had encountered. We had to take time off from work and arrange care for our other children in order to drive Bianca to each appointment. While we were consumed with all of this, the household still had to be managed, bills paid, work responsibilities continued and the boys needed our involvement and oversight. We couldn't put any of this on hold. There was no one who could take away the work, although friends and family did step in to help when needed. I did the best that I could under the circumstances. My notes, papers, memos to memory, IEP reports, counselor notes, hospital discharge paperwork, provider names and telephone numbers, school meetings, police reports, court documents,

DMH applications and group home progress reports were overflowing in boxes and file cabinets in our house. This trail of paper was testimony to all that Bianca and we had endured.

Given her well documented mental illness and placement into a group home, we were presented with the option of revoking her adoption and relinquishing custody to the Department of Children and Families (DCF). As awful as the past years had been, we were still going to help our daughter. We could not, in good conscience, walk away from parenthood when things got tough. We loved her deeply, even after everything she had put us through and especially after all that she had been through. Bianca needed a contained environment if she was going to get well. Our decision was firm; we would keep full custody. We would not revoke the adoption. Although we could no longer have her live safely at home, we were still her family, and I was still her mother. Yes, we had been living in a mental illness war zone, but I would not give her away.

With Bianca gone, the house was suddenly quiet and my next steps were to re-establish normalcy. The burden of caring for a child so sick had taken its toll on all of us. We had to stabilize our family and repair the trauma from the last three years. Our house had been in an uproar. The boys' school performance had dropped, and they both were more withdrawn and cautious. The situation had been hard for them. It was not easy to do well in school while dealing with a stressful environment at home. We survived as best we could, but the effects were showing on all of us. My blood pressure was high, and I was taking two medications to control it. Karl and I were exhausted and having difficulty sleeping. Our family had been living under siege for years. It was time to restore peace.

I had been barely able to keep up with the demands of running the house, working full-time and staying connected with family, friends and church. Our marriage was intact and hadn't cracked under the strain, but it had been hard. There were days when I didn't want to get out of bed. There were days when I am sure Karl did not want to come home. One morning, after little sleep, and feeling like I had been run over by a truck, Karl asked me how I was doing. I wanted to tell him how miserable I was, how tired, scared, angry and drained. I wanted to cry and run away. I didn't. Instead, I looked at my husband. There he was, exhausted himself, looking like hell, while trying to stay positive and worry about me. He could have taken his frustration out on me but never did. I paused before answering and realized that we were in this together, and I loved him because of everything we had been through. As awful as it was, we never gave up or blamed each other. We were a team. Somehow that morning, I found a deep inner strength and said, "I am doing all right, but this is hard and it has been awful. I'm tired." And then I asked, "How are you?" He said that he was doing "okay." We talked further. He admitted that he was tired and worried about Bianca and how it would all turn out. Then he smiled and said, "Let's make a dinner date night out. We need to do something fun this week." My mood brightened. I was glad that making time together was a priority.

I had forgotten how it felt to be normal. I had always kept myself healthy but life had been difficult the past few years, and I let go of many things as a result, including my fitness routine and diet. I struggled with house routines: Cleaning, yard work, grocery shopping, cooking, laundry and keeping up with all of the family appointments. Karl and I teamed up to tackle duties together, but the years of dealing with Bianca on top of everything else left me exhausted. I was not eating well and was having difficulty sleeping. I startled easily and was always on edge, waiting for the next outburst or fight. I couldn't relax, and I was having a hard time recovering. Looking back on this period, I realize now that I was suffering from post-traumatic stress disorder. But at the time, I was on autopilot, surviving each day and trying to move forward. I didn't have time to slow down. All of the demands of running a house did not go away. The things we "let go" while helping Bianca were waiting for our attention. We were under a mountain of work. It was going to take a lot of effort to dig ourselves out and a lot of time to repair the damage.

Karl and I somehow had managed to keep up with the demands of a growing family through all of Bianca's crises. We divided the work and took turns dealing with the boys' school issues. They were involved with many extra-curricular activities, including school, church, scouts, sports and time with friends. Our youngest son, Stephen, was completing his junior black belt, which required intense training and concentration. Our oldest son, Michael, had a part-time job, a girlfriend and a car, which kept us on our toes and ever vigilant. My husband and I were both working full-time in demanding careers. Our employers were understanding and accommodated our attendance at all of Bianca's appointments and meetings. Fortunately, I had a flexible schedule and was able to work evening hours as well as some weekends and holidays to make up for time off. In spite of the upheaval at home, our work performances did not suffer. Life remained busy and even though Bianca was not living under our roof, we were still very involved with her at Solace. We attended weekly family therapy sessions with her counselor, went to regular team meetings, DMH updates and various family-sponsored activities. We visited her often and regularly. I was grateful that Bianca was in a safe place getting treatment. And she was beginning to look better.

Bianca stabilized at Solace. She was safe and made progress with her school work. Our city agreed to pay for the education she was receiving there and amended the IEP accordingly. Counseling sessions helped her identify and manage her feelings without hurting herself or threatening others. Family work explored the impact of her mental illness and strengthened our relationship. It was intense and difficult. I was cautious. It was hard to open up and share my feelings. Out of necessity, I had learned to keep my emotions in check to manage Bianca's volatility. The counselor challenged me to examine myself and my parenting methods. Could I have done anything different? We were encouraged to tell each other how her illness affected us and how we were feeling about her living away. Bianca was usually hostile and angry during these sessions. She blamed me for putting her out of the house. All of the anger about being adopted and feeling abandoned mixed together with adolescent hormones and mental illness boiled over. I was the target of her rage. Everything I did to help her, the sadness about our broken home, the stress it had on me and on all of the family didn't make any difference. In her view, I represented everything that was wrong with her life.

I left sessions drained and sad. Sometimes I got angry. I did not regret the way that I parented. In fact, I believed that no one else could have dealt with Bianca and managed as well as I did. I put up with years of her abuse. I kept my marriage strong, attended to the needs of our children, managed the rigors of a professional career and maintained smooth household operations. It was trying, to say the least, to sit in a room while being under attack, but I held firm. Although I was open to suggestions, final parenting decisions were mine. I could live with the consequences. I felt that I had done a damn good job.

Counseling and questions about my parenting from someone who was just out of graduate school, was single and had never parented a mentally ill child required restraint. I did not want to appear defensive, but my life experience gave me a unique perspective that, quite frankly, a young clinician did not have. We had some powerful conversations and were able to respect each other's perspective. I realize the clinical staff had Bianca's best interest at heart, and asking tough questions was part of the treatment plan. I learned to put my ego aside and work with the therapy team. We even agreed to disagree. Slowly and over time, I began to see small gains from these therapy sessions as hard as they were to go through at the time.

The Solace staff was highly skilled. They navigated the emotional minefield of a house full of mentally ill adolescents. They aptly managed the daily drama, hurt feelings and turmoil of these helpless children. Solace was an oasis, and we all started to recover there. Bianca was safe and made progress under their care, and I was able to get my normal back. I have fond memories of the staff during our time together. They understood Bianca and did not judge her or me. I learned to put aside my need for perfection and appreciate small gains.

Bianca formed lasting relationships with some of the residents. These children had tragic circumstances that brought them to this place with bruised and wounded souls, which were the result of faulty genetics and bad luck. Being in their midst was a heartbreaking reminder of how vulnerable and misunderstood they were. I was beginning to see mental illness in a different light. This could happen to anyone's child and strike any family at any time. Mental illness is not a preventable disease. There is no cure or magic treatment to put it in remission. We "manage" it, but that involves a lot of trial and error. Patients receive prescriptions and wait to see which medication or cocktail combination will give the best results with the fewest side effects, always hoping for the right balance. Bianca was fortunate. Her medications were working with few side effects. As a result, she was able to focus on her treatment plan and make good progress.

She continued to do well in school and at the house. We were eventually allowed to take her off campus to explore nearby parks, pizza joints and downtown shops. It felt good to spend time together as a family. We visited every weekend with our dog. They were delighted to see each other, and this was good therapy for everyone. There were occasional moments of hostility and swearing; however, I was skilled at recognizing when Bianca's behavior was beginning to escalate and intervene to prevent it from getting out of control. We both were making progress with our relationship, and it was less tumultuous. As a result, I was able to avoid big blowouts and keep our visits on friendly terms.

Bianca's mood was stable, and she began to take special care with her hygiene and pay attention to looking nice. It was wonderful to see her beauty re-emerge. She loved to shop so we picked out fragrant body washes, shampoo and clothes while trying to keep within budget, striking the balance between want and need. The limit of family funds sometimes led to typical teen-parent disagreement; she wanted to buy more items than we could afford. It was hard for her to manage frustration when she couldn't buy everything she wanted. But these moments were infrequent and didn't last long. I was also happy to see glimpses of her kindness re-emerge. She was generous and often gave her clothes to other girls who did not have much. In therapy, she began to talk about how much her family meant to her and how much she missed being home. After many months of stabilization and progress at Solace, we got permission for Bianca to have her first overnight home pass.

She had not been home for over one year. I was worried that we would slip back into the familiar chaos of life before containment. I liked the peace and quiet of our home and did not want to disrupt it. Yet, I knew she couldn't remain away indefinitely. She had made progress and was stable now. It was time to take the next step. The overnight passes were rehearsed in advance so everyone knew what to expect, and they were time limited. We picked Bianca up from Solace on Saturday afternoon, ate dinner together, watched a little television, went to bed and returned her to the group home after church and lunch the following day. It was good to have family time at home but I was cautious. I was waiting to see how these visits would go. The boys held back and were careful to give her space, not knowing how she would behave. It had been a long time since we had been all together and even longer since we had fun together as a family. None of us knew what to expect, but I knew that we had to try to reconnect. This was a major milestone in our recovery. Family visits were for the most part peaceful, and there were no big blowouts. These first steps toward family reunification were a quiet success.

But by the time winter arrived, Bianca was not doing well. She was cutting again and went to the emergency room for sutures a few times. She also began to pierce herself. She pierced her eyebrows, upper and lower lips, tongue, ears, ear cartilage, chest, breast, navel, and abdomen. The cuttings and piercings were performed with whatever supplies were at hand: Paper clips, disassembled safety razors, pen caps, staples and safety pins. These wounds soon became infected, and she had to be treated with multiple antibiotics. There were several times when the infections spread to surrounding tissues, a dangerous condition called cellulitis, which required aggressive medical care.

I was scared for her health, imagining the worst: Nerve damage, deformity, drug resistant bacteria from exposure to so much antibiotic and even sepsis if the infection spread. Bianca was placed on a safety plan. Sharp objects, including all jewelry, were removed from her possession and she was searched every time she returned from school, group trip or family outing. She was not allowed a razor to shave. If she wanted to shave, she had to use an electric razor with a female staff member watching. These precautions did not stop the behavior, and she continued to find objects to cut and pierce. The psychiatrist adjusted her medication to try and inhibit the impulse to self-mutilate. It did not work right away, and weekend passes were temporarily placed on hold. Eventually, the medication changes took effect and the urge to cut and pierce subsided. Family overnight passes resumed, but we were not out of the woods. Bianca was angry that we would not allow her to visit a boyfriend from school. She badgered us to change our minds. She wanted us to drive her to his house. We explained why this was not allowed, as all passes were authorized by her counselor in advance. This visit was not part of the agreed upon weekend plan. Eventually, she stopped pestering us to change our minds. She went to bed angry but compliant. I was relieved to have settled the dispute without a big fight. The next morning, I woke up at my usual time and padded downstairs in robe and slippers to make coffee. A deep New England overnight freeze registered minus 10 degrees on the thermometer. As I entered the kitchen I felt a frigid blast. The back door was wide open, the furnace was roaring and the house was barely maintaining 40 degrees. After closing the door, I was reassured to see that everything was intact. We had not been robbed. But what about the children! I raced to their bedrooms.

Our teenage children usually slept until 11 o'clock on weekend mornings. This gave Karl and me much needed quiet alone time. This was our oasis until the first footsteps began the day. This schedule meant that they were up late at night. Sometimes we went to bed before the children once the house was secured and a final goodnight check was made. We tried to stay awake until after they went to bed, but this wasn't always possible. As a result, we usually didn't get much sleep on weekends.

I was relieved when I entered the boys' bedrooms. They were both sleeping soundly and emitted reassuring soft snores. As I entered Bianca's bedroom, I found that the light was on. I wasn't alarmed as this was usual because of her fear of the dark. The mound of blankets in the middle of the bed looked like she was curled up underneath. Again, this was typical for her. I gingerly peeked under the covers as I didn't want to disturb her, but she was not in her bed. I threw back the covers to make sure she wasn't curled at the foot of the bed. My heart began to race and suddenly I felt like I was going to be sick. I yelled to Karl and looked around her room. The closet was open. Her weekend bag, pocketbook, jacket, sneakers, makeup and hair brush were missing.

We raced through the house and looked everywhere: In closets, on couches, behind furniture and every inch of every room, including the basement and the garage. We methodically scoured the house again to be sure she wasn't hiding or sleeping in an unusual place. We put our boots and jackets on and looked outside for clues: Footprints in the snow, cigarette butts in the driveway, tire tracks or other clues to help us determine what had happened. There was no trace of her anywhere. We looked and looked again just to be sure we hadn't missed anything. With each step, that sick, sinking feeling got worse. Bianca was not home. At the age of 15 she had run away. She was gone. We did not know where she was, who she was with, what she was doing or if she was safe.

I fought back rising hysteria and tried to think clearly. Was this an impulse? The back door was left open on one of the coldest nights of the year. That was not usual for Bianca. She was always careful to close doors, usually with a bang. We didn't hear a door slam in the night. What about the missing personal items and suitcase? This indicated that she had planned to leave. Who picked her up? She was too young to drive, and none of her friends had licenses or cars. Did she go to visit the boyfriend? We looked on her Facebook page and telephone log. Nothing unusual was posted or sent. *Dear God*, I thought, *this is a nightmare. Help her. Help us. Please keep her safe.*

We called the group home. The staff followed protocol and notified the administrator on call. They knew just what to do. They would file the necessary reports with DMH headquarters and notify the local police. We were instructed to look on her Facebook page for clues and post that we loved her and to please come home — no questions asked. We were told to message her contacts via Facebook and cell phone requesting information and help locating her. We called our family, our pastor and friends to let them know what had happened. We asked each one if they had heard from her and to pray for her safe return. We also asked that they let us know if they learned anything.

I was worried because Bianca left all of her medication behind. These prescriptions stabilized her mood, depression, impulses and anxiety. She had already missed her morning doses and would be starting to withdraw. She would be coming off her medication "cold-turkey" and without supervision, and the physical effects could be dire. The phone continued to ring; our pastor, family and friends offered words of comfort. Was there anything they could do? How could they help? They asked us to call the minute we heard anything and they would call us, as well. They all sent their love and prayers.

We had no idea where our daughter was, who she was with or what she was doing. Unable to eat or function, we reviewed events leading up to this moment. What did we miss? How did this happen? What do we do next? DMH called and instructed us to go to our police station and file a missing person report. We did not have to wait until she had been gone for 24 hours as she was a minor with a psychiatric history and was on DMH caseload. She was an at-risk runaway child in a residential group home. Solace called back to report that their interviews with residents were negative. No one knew anything. They also placed calls to parents of residents on weekend leave as well as day student families. Did anyone know if Bianca made plans, they were asked? Did they hear anything? Everyone was concerned but unable to offer anything helpful. Solace promised to let us know the minute they had news.

Karl and I waited. We scoured her cell phone history. We read messages and looked for familiar or frequently called numbers. When was the last time she used her phone? What was the time, and what numbers did she call? her last phone call was the previous night after 10 o'clock. It was frequently listed in the log. I wrote the number down on a piece of paper and dialed. There was no answer, and it did not go to voicemail. In the meantime, she did not return our calls or pleading texts — "Please tell us that you're okay. Let us know where you are so we can bring you home. We are not mad. We are worried. We love you," we told her.

We looked on Facebook. There were no suspicious messages. Bianca shared a few exchanges with a boy named John. The school called back. They had information that she might be with a boy named John. They were still waiting for more calls to be returned but were able to give us John's last name. He and Bianca were friends in school and were in the same grade. We went to the police station with this information and filed a missing person report of a child at risk. We included a physical description of her, including height and weight, special markings, piercings and tattoos. We gave them a recent picture, her history, the school name, number and contact person. They entered her information into the database, but there wasn't a child fitting Bianca's description in it. We gave them John's name. Within minutes they produced a picture and asked if we had ever seen the person before. It was the same picture we saw on her Facebook. It matched his information from school. Armed with the positive identification, the police notified the law enforcement in John's hometown. They would assist with the search. Hopeful with this promising lead, we went home to wait.

There is nothing worse than a missing child. The terror of not knowing if your child is alive, hurt or lost is excruciating. Minutes drag into hours. Without information you visit dark places and try not to drown. We had been working in a frenzy since early morning. We prayed hard and did our best to hold on. I had to keep calm for the boys' sake. It would do no good to cave in. I had to be strong no matter what. There was nothing left to do. I put on a brave face and, as the hours passed, waited for the police to find our daughter.

I am thankful for these officers. We were fortunate to have their support when dealing with her. They were experienced with children like Bianca, understood behavior and gave sound advice on how to deal with it. I listened and learned from the front-line officers assisting her in crisis as well as her probation officer and court officials. I followed their advice and kept them informed of our progress and setbacks. I always had a connection with someone who could help, and we never had a bad experience. I encourage anyone with a child in crisis to connect immediately with these professionals. They are open 24/7 and do not require a co-payment or prior authorization to access their expertise and services.

By late afternoon, the Dracut police found Bianca at John's house. She was unharmed but furious at being found. I never found out where John's mother was during this time or if she was home or aware that her underage son had a girlfriend spend the night. She could not return to the group home until she was cleared by a psychiatrist and drug test. We picked her up at the police station, signed paperwork and drove her to the nearest emergency room. Someone from the house staff met us there. By eight o'clock, she was cleared and discharged into the care of the group home. We went home.

The remainder of the year was quiet. Weekend passes were resumed once the event was processed and she agreed to follow rules. There were a few outbursts at school and in the group home: Bullying, gossip drama, defiance, swearing, borrow-steal misunderstandings and so forth. But these were minor events and aptly managed by staff. Bianca did manage to get into trouble during a field trip. She made disrespectful comments to a few of the local "townies." They got mad and gave chase, threatening to beat her up. She was scared and ran back to the safety of the group. The incident ended without harm. From that time forward, we could not get her to go with us to shop, walk or eat there.

The respite from drama lasted a few months. She was doing well in school and with counseling and was no longer cutting or piercing herself. There were no outbursts or defiant acts at Solace or at home. We were pleased that she was stable and made good progress overall since her admission there. But I was unprepared for the chain of events that were about to transpire.

"I am in Lynn and I want to come home." The phone call came at one o'clock in the morning, jolting us awake.

"How in the world did you get to Lynn?" She was home on a weekend pass and we thought she was in bed. "Go to the nearest police station," we directed. "Where are you?"

"I don't know. I'm cold and scared," Bianca said.

"Describe what you see. Are there any street or business signs?"

We got out the road map. Based on her description of nearby landmarks and our knowledge of the city, we were able to give directions to the police. It was quicker for her to walk, as it would take us 30 minutes to get to her. She agreed. The police called while we were getting dressed. She was safe. She was cold but unharmed. She had gone to a party and when she wanted to leave, there was no transportation home. "Friends" had picked her up at the end of our driveway while we were asleep. Even though I am a light sleeper, she left the house so quietly, I didn't hear a thing.

Because Bianca had been unsupervised and away from our care while on a pass, she could not return to the group home without another screen at a hospital. We were familiar with this routine. Karl left the police station and drove her to the emergency room. Once again, Solace staff met him there. He returned home in the early morning pre-dawn hours. We were exhausted and went back to bed. We slept in that Sunday, skipped church and got up with the boys before noon. It had been a long night.

Soon after Bianca returned to Solace, she began to smell. Her personal hygiene took a sharp turn for the worse. The smell from her feet and private areas was horrific. She seemed unaware of this and when it was brought to her attention, she was dismissive and unconcerned. "I don't care," she said. The staff began a reward system every time she took a bath, shampoo and put on clean clothes. It helped a little but in the meantime, she resumed the piercings to her eyebrow, nose, upper and lower lip, ears and ear cartilage, breast, chest and abdomen. There were also sharp cuts incised on her thighs and forearms. The piercings got infected again, requiring trips to the physician for medical care. The prescribed antibiotics and wound care required constant vigilance by the staff at Solace. Bianca didn't care if she took the antibiotics or not. She removed her bandages and picked at her scabs. She ripped her clothes and cut them with scissors.

One day, we went to the mall during an afternoon pass. She wanted to spend her Christmas money and buy a few clothes and cosmetics. I thought this was a good idea, pleased that she was paying attention to looking nice again. We agreed to meet in 30 minutes. As Bianca walked away, I heard her say, "Let's get down to business." I thought she meant it was time to do some shopping. What I didn't know was that she was planning to shoplift. When she returned to the group home, they found items without a sales receipt. I suspected that she may have stuffed these items beneath legitimate purchases. The items were returned and family passes were restricted again. To complicate matters, the girls at Solace swapped clothes. When Bianca wore a new outfit that we didn't purchase, she said that she traded for the clothes or that they were a gift from a friend. Solace prohibited swapping or sharing items among residents because of the conflict that typically arose from such arrangements.

Despite the ups and downs, Bianca was relatively stable overall. With the arrival of spring in 2011, she was completing her second year at Solace and was assigned a new counselor, her third. Each one was well qualified but had a different style, requiring a period of adjustment until she became familiar with them and comfortable with their approach. It was not easy to adjust to someone new. The transition of new staff unraveled the status quo, causing more distress and acting out. Her behavior, though manageable, was not stable and these transitions did not help. As a result, she ramped up verbal and physical altercations in school and at the residence. The police were called a few times. She was able to calm down with their arrival, and she was never arrested or charged with a crime because she did not damage property or assault anyone. She was suspended from classes and placed on house confinement after each incident.

The new counselor recommended an independent evaluation from a specialist in the DMH because there was concern that Bianca was becoming institutionalized. They thought that at the age of 17, she should begin to transition out of a controlled environment and move into a program that would allow her to re-enter the community. We were also told that Solace was changing from a long-term group home to a short-term stabilization program. There was a pressing need to increase the number of available residential beds in the state. More children would be served by quickly turning over occupancy at Solace and decreasing the length of stay. I understood the rationale for the recommendation although I was concerned that in light of Bianca's recent behavior, it might be a premature plan.

It was time for her to re-engage with society, they said. The decision was made. She would move to a group home where she would have more freedom. She could learn to be independent in the community with their support. The new program would help her reach the developmental milestones that she missed from being away for so long. She would learn to take public transportation, get her license and find a job. I was reassured that the program was successful but urged that time was of the essence. Bianca would leave Solace at the end of the school year and settle into the new program over the summer. In the fall, she would return to Solace for classes during the day. She would complete her high school education and graduate in the spring of 2013 when she was 19. We packed her belongings and said goodbye to the Solace staff who had been our family for two years. Bianca was excited for a change and was looking forward to more freedom. The future was a mystery, and none of us had any idea what was coming. I hoped we were making the right move, but when all was said and done we didn't have any other choice.

chapter **4**

FROM BAD TO WORSE

The Highway was a stately Victorian-style house situated on top of a hill overlooking the city of Lynn. This was to be Bianca's new home, and she was thrilled that she was assigned to her very own room. After years of sharing space with other girls, she finally had the privacy she craved. The house staff took pride in showing us all of the rooms. The formal living and dining rooms commanded spectacular views of the city and ocean beyond.

When we arrived, the house was empty of residents, since everyone was working or at school. The furniture, drapes and thick carpets were immaculately maintained. I was impressed, to say the least. The intake was a long process, one that we had been through many times before and were accustomed to. We sat in the living room for several hours reviewing all of Bianca's information and goals for the Highway program. She would continue with school at Solace. The bus would pick her up at 6:15 in the morning and drive her to Ipswich 15 miles away. Bianca would enter the 11th grade and even though she had been dealing with mental illness all these years, she had kept up with her class. She was a whiz at math and loved expressive arts and cooking. She was excited that Highway offered the opportunity to attend evening cooking classes at the community college in town. Bianca was a good cook. She made custards, decorated cakes, baked homemade bread, stir-fried Kung pao shrimp and often cooked meals for us and the residents at Solace. I was hopeful that she would do well and take advantage of the opportunities there.

The Highway was designed to support residents while they learned how to go into the city, shop, walk in parks, attend school and work. These privileges were given for good behavior such as personal hygiene, room cleanliness, following rules, helping with chores, meeting with counselors and keeping appointments. Excursions into the city required a buddy with a specific destination, check-in and return time. Trips to the park, a strip mall and burger joint down the street reinforced responsibility and safety. Certain areas of the city were off limits because they were dangerous. Rules were clear and non-negotiable. Bianca signed the contract, a memorandum of understanding of house rules and agreement with the education plan.

After a few weeks Bianca was given her first day pass. She was thrilled with this new freedom and diligently followed all of the rules to get this privilege. I was impressed with her effort and relieved that the passes were a success. Within a few weeks, however, she was placed on house arrest. She broke curfew and did not check in, answer phone calls or return to the Highway on time. As a result, she had to go to the local emergency room for a psychiatric screening and drug test. The toxicology report showed a small amount of marijuana and nicotine in her blood. I was disappointed that this happened and at the same time relieved that she was safe and didn't have anything stronger in her system. She processed the event with staff and said that she realized the importance of following rules for safety. Bianca was testing new boundaries, seeing what she could get away with and discovering freedom.

The Highway assigned Bianca a new psychiatrist to prescribe her medications. We met the nurse in residence, counselor, program director and the rest of the house staff. Everyone was cheerful and professional. I was impressed again at the resources put in place to support her; everyone was committed to helping her be successful. Appointments were made for a physical exam, eye testing and dental care. She was prescribed glasses for reading. This was the first pair of eyeglasses and she joked that she looked "wicked smart." She said that reading was easier now, and we thought that some of the school difficulties may have been caused, in part, by limited vision. The orthodontia work was finally completed after four years. It had been a long process beginning with the extraction of four teeth to make room for overcrowding. The dental work should have been finished sooner but was delayed due to non-compliance from mental illness. She usually refused to brush her teeth, which led to arguments.

"Bianca, did you brush your teeth?"
"Yeah," came the bored reply.

"Well, the toothbrush is dry, how is that possible?" I asked, as she slammed her bedroom door and shouted, "Get off my fucking back!"

Trying to remain calm, I appealed to her sense of reason through the closed door.

"Well, the plaque has lots of bacteria that will grow unless you brush and you will get cavities."
"Fuck you!" was her reply.

Her toothbrush remained dry.

We had endured emergency trips to the orthodontist to repair broken wires as well as several root canals to preserve her front tooth damaged from the playground mishap so long ago. Bianca had a few cavities filled along the way and continued to struggle with oral hygiene, but the day that her braces were removed, she stepped into the waiting room with a big beautiful smile. I realized that in the midst of mental illness she had grown into a beautiful young woman and that all of our hair-pulling efforts to complete the dental work had been worth it.

To celebrate the removal of braces, I treated Bianca to a manicure, hair cut, color and styling. Afterwards we ate lunch and went shopping for summer clothes. It was a lovely afternoon, and we enjoyed our time together. The tension between us was gone that day. This is how mothers and daughters were meant to be, I thought — comfortable with each other and happy. It had been such a long time since we were able to be like this that I had forgotten how nice it felt. She was thrilled with the outing, and I was happy with the clothes she selected. They were stylish, pretty and complimented her figure. I was confident that she was in a good program that was meeting her needs. We kissed goodbye and made plans to get together the following weekend for a lunch date and walk.

"Bye, Mommy, thank you for a great day. See you next week. I love you." Her words carried me as I drove home.

The following week, Bianca attempted to have sex with one of the male residents. It was not successful because the liaison in the bathroom was intercepted by staff. She then broke another rule by not answering her phone or checking in with staff while out. Once again, she was required to go to the hospital for a mental health screening and drug test. She followed the standard operating procedure without complaint. She was unfazed and knew the routine: Wait for the ambulance and go to the local emergency room with staff; receive a DMH mental health assessment for risk of self-harm and review the event with her Highway counselor, program director and DMH outreach counselor. The DMH visited Bianca for several days afterward for support and to help prevent another incident. She was a quick study and had learned the system already. She said all the right things to get what she wanted since there were no real consequences, just temporary inconveniences and a second chance later. Every time she failed to check in or come home on time, we paid the price waiting for news from the Highway that she had returned and was safe.

One night, we were awakened by the phone. It was after 10 o'clock. I struggled to make sense of what I was hearing. The Highway was calling to inform us that Bianca was gone.

It was August 10, 2011 and this time the call was different.

She had left the Highway at approximately 8 o'clock, and staff had been trying to locate her without success. No one knew where she was, and she was not returning any phone calls. One of the residents reported that as he was sitting on the front steps smoking a cigarette, she brushed by him and said "goodbye." She then proceeded across the lawn to greet a young woman who stepped out of a small red car as Bianca approached. They got into the back seat together and the car immediately drove away. He could not give a good description of the car or the license plate number because it was dark. He did not recognize the girl or the driver and could not provide any other details. The Highway staff sprang into action. They notified the administrator on call, the local police, DMH headquarters and us. We checked Bianca's cell phone and Facebook home page. There was no phone activity since 8 o'clock and nothing posted on Facebook. We had no information.

Once again, we were shoved into a parent's worst nightmare. Our daughter was gone, and no one knew where she was or who she was with or even if she was safe. She was not returning calls. Her cell phone immediately went to voicemail, indicating that it had been turned off. We left messages on her phone and Facebook. The staff had no leads. We heard nothing. Bianca had walked away from the Highway and vanished without a trace or clue. I tried to remain calm and put on a brave face, clinging to hope and praying that she was safe. We didn't do very well that night. I fought rising hysteria as the hours ticked by without any news. We couldn't sleep and, given the late hour, did not call our friends or family for support. We were all alone with our fears. I kept my terror to myself, not wanting to add to Karl's distress. Helpless to do anything, we waited. As dawn approached, I brewed a pot of coffee to combat the effects of no sleep and braced myself for the new day.

On Thursday, we waited and talked with the Highway staff throughout the day. We notified our family and friends and tried not to cause unnecessary alarm. It didn't work. Everyone tried to help and offer support, but there was nothing anyone could do except wait. There was no contact from Bianca that day. The police had little information to go on and were unable to offer any assistance other than to post a missing person alert. I dragged myself to work after little sleep and tried to stay busy and distracted. We went through the usual evening routine that night, trying to maintain normalcy and order. Our lives had been dumped into the endless cycles of gut-wrenching panic, worry and fear of the unknown. Where was our daughter? Unable to eat or sleep, I imagined the worst. The minutes dragged into endless hours without any information. It was hard to hold onto sanity. The wait was excruciating.

Friday morning came and we still had no news. We waded through another exhausting day of work, and I went through the motions as best as I could. I could not sit still. The silence and lack of information was awful, and I coped by staying busy. I cleaned, scrubbed, dusted, vacuumed and did laundry all day Saturday — anything to occupy my mind. This was our third day without any information about Bianca. We kept checking her Facebook page and telephone log, but they were empty and without activity. Something was desperately wrong. She was always on her phone and Facebook. We posted messages and left more voicemails on her phone. We texted her friends, pleading for information, a word, a message, anything. The boys were concerned but not overly worried. They had been through so much, living with their sister's drama and turmoil and were adept at shielding themselves. I was a wreck. I was nauseous, anxious and unable to keep food down. Rest was impossible. Karl fared no better. He paced, ate little, didn't sleep and spent hours poring over her phone records and Facebook page. Eerily quiet, he seemed to grow thinner and became more withdrawn with each passing day.

The following morning, Sunday, a phone call came through on the house phone from a number that we did not recognize. At that point, we were answering any and all telephone calls. This one stopped us cold. It was Bianca. Her voice was faint and sounded so far away. She said she was tired and in a small quivering voice said, "I want to come home."

"Where are you? Tell us where you are," I practically yelled into the phone. "We will come and get you."

She said that she was in Fall River, Massachusetts and was calling from a telephone in the lobby of a motel. She knew the name of the place but not the street address. She did not have her pocketbook, cell phone or shoes.

"Are you alone?" I asked.

"No." she replied. "There is a lady at the desk. She let me use the phone, but I can't stay here."

We asked her to look around to see if there was a business that was open nearby.

"Yes, there's a Shell gas station across the street."

"Good," I said. "Go there right now and tell the people who work at the gas station that you are lost and that your father is on his way to come and get you. Give them our name and telephone numbers. We are coming to that address right now. We'll be there in one hour. Stay at the gas station. Don't go anywhere else, no matter what. Get out of the motel right now."

We raced to get ready. I packed a bag of toiletries, clothes, shoes, food and water for Bianca. We notified the Highway, and they in turn notified the police and DMH. We were instructed to bring her to the hospital after we picked her up and staff would meet us there. Karl plugged the address into the GPS and left. I stayed behind to wait for news and take care of the boys.

Eventually, the anxiously awaited telephone call came through. Bianca was safe in the car, and they were driving to the hospital. I spoke to her briefly. She said she was tired and glad that her father had come to pick her up. Hearing her voice was a huge relief. She was safe! I collapsed into the chair, exhausted and overcome. We had our daughter back and she was alive. This was such wonderful news, but I still had so many questions that needed answers. How did this happen, why did this happen and what happened while she was missing? As the morning dragged into the afternoon, Karl called. The house staff was at the hospital and Bianca would be discharged to the Highway shortly. He was coming home. By then it was late afternoon. Many hours had passed when the car turned into our driveway, but he was home.

While seated at the kitchen table, exhausted and drained, we drank cups of tea and talked late into the evening. Bianca had been dirty, barefoot, exhausted, hungry and thirsty when Karl picked her up. She hadn't eaten in days. She was sitting in front of the gas station on a curb by the side of the street. Several men had come by while she was waiting and asked if she wanted money or a ride. She might have said yes before, but now tired and afraid, she just wanted to go home and declined their offers. She hadn't slept in days. Karl told her story and I struggled to comprehend his words.

Our worst nightmare had come true. Our beautiful daughter had been kidnapped, raped and forced into prostitution. Bianca was a victim of human trafficking: A slave controlled and sold for profit without consent. She had been raped at gunpoint by the man who kidnapped her and drove the red car. Bianca thought she was going to a party with a girl she met on Facebook. There was no party. She had been tricked to get her away from the group home. The friend was a victim of human trafficking herself and received a "bonus" for bringing girls into prostitution for her pimp. The bonus gave time off from turning tricks, pocket change, clean clothes, a shower, food and rest. As soon as Bianca arrived at the apartment and realized there was no party, her pocketbook, shoes and cell phone were taken away. The apartment was locked, and she was pushed into a dirty bedroom. The man followed and held a gun to her head while he raped her. After the rape, she was drugged and locked in the apartment. Over the course of three days men came into the apartment and paid the pimp for sex with the captives. She was not given food but was able to drink water from the bathroom faucet.

There were several young girls there, too. One girl was as

young as 11 or 12. They were not allowed to speak to each other and were kept in separate rooms. All were drugged and raped repeatedly by a stream of men over several days and nights, deprived of sleep, hygiene and food. Sunday morning, she realized that the apartment door was unlocked, and she quickly slipped out of the apartment and ran into the lobby where there was an attendant and a phone. It was a miracle that she escaped and was alive. Our hearts were broken and we cried together, shattered by the reality of what had happened to our daughter. It was a sad, sad day.

Human sex trafficking is a thriving underground business that preys on children. Trafficking is a violation of federal civil rights laws and, sadly, two million children are exploited every year in global commercial sex trade. Child trafficking victims come from all backgrounds, racial groups and from both rural and city areas. It is a business driven by profit. If nobody paid for sex, it would cease to exist. Bianca got into a car because she knew a girl and thought they were going to a party. They were not friends but only acquaintances through a mutual friend — a friend of a friend — and chatted on social media. There were other girls at the "party," and they were given alternative names. Her "friend" was also a victim but had more privileges. When she slipped out the door and begged to use a phone, the kind clerk didn't turn her away. That act and the fact that we answered her call immediately probably saved her life.

Later that evening, we received a call from the Highway. Bianca was suicidal, threatening to kill herself and was being brought to the hospital. Staff remained with her, and we were kept up to date throughout the night and into the next day. She was not safe to be discharged back to the Highway and needed in-patient psychiatric care. By early afternoon the following day a bed had been found. We packed some clothes and basic toiletries and went to see her. The routine of these visits was all too familiar. We were able to meet with her briefly in a small conference room. Guests were required to leave all possessions in a locker prior to entering the unit and were allowed 20 minutes for visits. Standard operating procedure required that all belongings brought into the unit were thoroughly searched for contraband, including drugs or items that could be used for harm. Cell phones were prohibited as were keys, pens, razors, belts or anything that could cause injury. The psychiatric ward had a double lock door system to keep patients from escaping. Bianca was happy to see us although she appeared heavily sedated. We told her that we loved her.

"I love you guys, too," came her reply.

"We will get through this together," I said.

All of our hearts were broken. We could only imagine what she had endured. I was enraged, scared and very sad. I wanted revenge but knew that this would not help anyone so I suppressed my feelings. There was no other choice. I reminded her that she was strong to have escaped and call for help. Her feelings were normal. She was safe.

Because Bianca was a victim of a crime, the hospital was required to notify the police. A detective and officer met with her when her psychiatrist said it was safe to do so. I worried that this would cause more trauma by reliving what had happened. She wanted to cooperate and I was proud of her, but she was afraid for the young girl in the apartment and worried about what she was experiencing. She wanted to help the other girls and hoped that her testimony would help the police find the man and free them. She didn't want anyone else to go through what she had. I was impressed with Bianca's strength. She did not waver and was able to give a statement and positively identify the man from a photo array. The police listened to her story and asked gentle but probing questions to get all of the facts correct. It was excruciating to hear the details of her rape and forced prostitution, but Bianca wanted us with her during the interview so we listened and tried not to cry.

The police reviewed next steps. They would issue a warrant for the arrest. Her story and identification corroborated a statement from a previous victim. This prostitution ring had been active for some time and was known to law enforcement, although they did not have enough information to make arrests until then. We were given instructions to get rid of all contact information from the cell phone and Facebook and not have any communication with the "friend" who lured Bianca away. We gave police the business address where Karl picked her up. That information, along with the description of the building was a strong lead. The police found and arrested the pimp. The officers were kind and understanding during the investigation and kept us informed. I was once more impressed with the sensitivity they showed to Bianca. There was no judgment, only kindness.

The Highway determined that their placement was not a good fit for her to continue living there any longer. They could not keep her safe because she continued to run away and break house rules. DMH scheduled an emergency meeting at headquarters. There were anxious looks and fidgeting from the Highway staff and DMH. Karl and I had initially agreed with their recommendation to place Bianca in the Highway, as it was supposed to help her learn to be independent and become less institutionalized. While it was a good idea in the beginning, it had turned into a colossal failure. She had run away, broken rules, ignored curfew and had been to the emergency room countless times. The kidnapping was the final straw. She could not go back to the Highway and she could not go back to Solace, either. While she was at the Highway, Solace had changed bed occupancy to short-term residence.

The Highway staff packed Bianca's belongings and met us at the hospital. We loaded her suitcase and several garbage bags stuffed with clothes and bedding into the car. After signing all of the discharge paperwork we drove west along Route 2 to her new home, the Dickens Home for Girls in the quaint town of Bernardston. She was resigned to yet another move and didn't complain. She was withdrawn and offered little in the way of conversation during the long ride, but she did not appear worried or anxious about another move to a strange place.

When we arrived, I was struck with how beautiful the house and grounds were. Bianca had a welcome basket waiting on her bed from the local women's club. It contained toiletries, robe, slippers, sheets and towels. Her room was charming as were the architectural details of the house. The rooms were decorated with comfortable chairs and couches and soft indirect lighting from tastefully arranged lamps that cast a warm glow. The effect was soothing - it felt like a cozy home instead of a group house.

She spent the next nine months there. We visited every weekend and discovered local walks, restaurants and shopping places. The downtown was within walking distance and was a nice destination for our family outings. Bianca made gains in the school on campus and was well on her way toward completing the 11th grade. She also was stabilized with her medication and therapy regimen. The added bonus at Dickens was that there were no boys to distract her, and she got along well with the other girls. With the element of boy distraction removed from the environment, she was able to focus on her studies, get good grades and make progress with her therapy. There were no further incidents of running away or fights at the Dickens. It was a good year.

As her birthday approached, we faced the reality that once she turned 18 in April, she would be considered a legal adult and, as such, would be in charge of her treatment. We met with the counselors and house staff to plan the next steps and prepare Bianca and us for this transition. In the meantime, because she had done so well at Dickens, she moved to a less structured home, the Rolf, which was located on the opposite side of town. The Rolf was similar to the Highway program and allowed residents to earn passes for good behavior. Once again, she had more freedom there and was able to attend evening classes, go shopping and walk downtown. I felt that Bernardston was safer to walk in than Lynn and was reassured that Bianca was not going to repeat the "get-into a car driven by a stranger to go to a party" scenario from the previous summer. She did well at the Rolf and followed all of the rules while she was there. I thought she had found the right combination of structure balanced with freedom, and given the lessons learned from the Highway, it was a safe place for her to live and complete her senior year of high school.

As her birthday neared, Bianca decided that she would not remain at the Rolf. She was adamant that she was going to leave on her birthday. She wanted to come home and attend the high school in our town to complete her senior year. The staff, counselor, DMH and we did not think this was a good idea and worried that she could get into trouble without the structure and therapeutic setting offered through the Rolf.

She was finally doing well and making progress with therapy and school. Why risk all of her success and hard work when she could safely stay for one more year and finish school? We explained and attempted to reason with her, but she didn't care. We were helpless to convince her otherwise. As a legal adult, she could make her own decisions regardless of our opinion. As parents, we felt obligated to support her even though we were terrified with her decision. The best we could hope for was that she would continue to do well and learn to be more independent. We had no choice. Our hands were tied. She was competent and legally free to make her own decisions as an adult. Bianca was clear; she would sign out of the group home and DMH care on her birthday. She would pack her bags and wait on the sidewalk for a ride. If we didn't pick her up, she would get a ride from a friend.

When her birthday arrived, Bianca agreed to postpone her exit for one week in order for the Rolf staff to finalize her discharge papers. Once again, all of her possessions were packed and loaded into the car. She signed all of the paperwork, received her discharge papers, cell phone and prescriptions. We were on our own. She had signed out of residence, school and DMH care. As we drove away, Bianca asked, "Am I really coming home now?"

"Yes," we replied. She turned pale and immediately vomited. After a few minutes, she recovered, overcome with emotion at the prospect of coming home after so many years. She remained pale and said that she felt better. After a quick stop at the nearest convenience store, I went inside and bought paper towels, plastic bags, carpet cleaner, Lysol and air freshener. We parked the car in the lot and attempted to clean the back seat. On the ride home, Bianca was texting.

"Drop me off at Sam's house," she said. "I'm going to stay there. It's okay. His mom said I could."

A heated argument followed and she told us that if we didn't drop her off at his house, she would hitch a ride there instead. This was not the first that I had heard of Sam. Bianca met him online and discovered that they already knew each other through a mutual friend in town. We drove to Sam's address and were greeted by Sam and his mother. They were happy to see Bianca and we made brief introductions, receiving assurances that she was welcome there. I was relieved that she had a nice boyfriend and family. I would have preferred that she come home instead but did not want to start another argument. We kissed goodbye. Other than the brief argument, the day had gone better than expected. She was happy and safe, and we had survived this turn of events without a big fight.

"This isn't so bad. We can do this," I told Karl.

Over the summer, Bianca established a pattern of visiting us at home. She and Sam would drive to the house for dinner, swim in the pool and leave before dark. On weekends they arrived mid-afternoon. They didn't usually stay for long and soon were off to visit a friend or go for a ride. She talked about going back to high school in the fall but didn't follow through with the plan.

By the end of the summer, Bianca was fighting with Sam's mother and sister. There were many heated arguments and angry phone calls until finally she was asked to leave. I was relieved and thought we would be better able to help her begin school and find a part-time job if she were living under our roof. In August, she moved back home and settled into her old bedroom. It was good to have her home.

Meanwhile, Sam was unemployed and looking for work. I wasn't sure when he had the time to go job hunting as he was always at our house. He would show up after breakfast and leave after dinner. He and Bianca would hang out, cook food, eat snacks, watch television, swim and walk the dog. They did not get into trouble or create a mess, so I didn't complain. I was glad that he was polite and kind to her. They seemed happy and, most importantly, she was stable and doing well.

We hired a tutor because she decided that she would not return to high school and wanted to complete her GED instead. One of her third grade summer school teachers was available and agreed to help. Mrs. Clough was one of our favorite teachers. She was patient and understood students with emotional as well as learning problems. Bianca and she had a good relationship in the past and now, many years later, shared an immediate connection. Weekly sessions were scheduled at the library, and she went to them willingly at first. Then, she began to "forget" to complete her homework so Mrs. Clough would help her finish it. Unfortunately, this cut down on instruction time for new material. The next excuse was that she was too tired to go, didn't sleep the night before or didn't feel well. I would leave work to pick her up and bring her to tutoring as arranged, but she would not be home. After a while she refused to go to her appointment.

"It's boring. I'll study and do it on my own," she would say.

Bianca had one excuse after another and reasons why she could not meet with Mrs. Clough or continue her education. I could do nothing else. I had gone out of my way to arrange for tutoring and transportation during my work hours. It was difficult to watch this educational opportunity slip away, but I forced myself to realize and face the fact that the decision to work toward the GED was hers alone. I was helpless to influence or change her mind. I could not force her to study.

While the halfhearted tutoring attempts were happening, Sam's car developed engine trouble, and he did not have the money to repair it so the car sat in his parents' driveway. His mother helped with his transportation problem and drove him to our house every day, dropping him off while we were at work. I came home after a long day to find Sam and Bianca asleep on the couch. Usually, the television was blaring and the lights were on. It was hard to wake them up.

I was not pleased. They were unemployed, high school dropouts and completely dependent on parental support.

They made no effort to change their situation, and encouragement or suggestions for improvement fell on deaf ears. They were missing the developmental milestones of young adulthood, education and work. The days were spent hanging out without goals or direction for the future. Bianca's lack of ambition was infuriating, and she was not setting a good example for her younger brother who was still in school. Discussions led to arguments and I was getting nowhere. Bianca resisted all attempts to encourage her to do something: Volunteering, tutoring, enrolling in school, taking cooking classes or even looking for a job. I told her we would pay for classes, support and bring her to interviews or work, but I could not change her mind or make her do anything. She was stuck, not moving forward with her future and not willing to change.

Bianca's erratic, moody behavior escalated and her sleep-wake cycles flipped. She was up during the night cooking or watching television and sleeping during the day. The smell of frying food woke me up in the middle of the night. Groggy and half asleep, I asked her to please finish cooking and go to bed because it was late and she was keeping me awake. My request was ignored.

"I'm almost done. What's your problem?" she would say, "Go back to bed."

The clatter of pans and banging cabinets intensified, daring me to respond. Better to leave her alone when she was in a mood like this, I concluded. I didn't have the energy to talk with her. It was late and the conversation would turn into a fight. In bed, I covered my head with a pillow and waited for her to finish.

In the morning, Bianca was sleeping when my alarm went off. The remains from the night before were left behind: Pans, leftover food and dirty dishes on the counter, bowls of unfinished milk and cereal dumped in the sink, which was now clogged with half-eaten sandwiches, salsa, eggs and peanut butter toast. Spills on the stove, counter and floor were left to dry and harden. Lights were on, faucets dripped, the refrigerator door was ajar and wet towels and dirty clothes were strewn in the bathroom along with puddles and gobs of toothpaste, hair gel and body wash.

Bianca remained in bed until Sam arrived. They would hang out in the television room, grab food when hungry, bring it back to eat and sleep on the couch for most of the day. They smoked in the driveway or on the deck. Cigarette butts were left in my garden beds, extinguished amongst the deck plants, thrown on the lawn or dropped in the driveway. They cooked and ate freely. There was a trail of dishes, clothes and wet towels throughout the house. Bianca's bedroom was strewn with dirty clothes, discarded food wrappers, drinks, half-eaten snacks, wet towels, cups and dirty dishes with dried, stuck-on food. She went through the motions of bathing, but it looked like the soap and water didn't touch her skin. Everything smelled.

I cleaned the fallout twice a day - in the morning before I left for work and again when I got home. When I tried to talk with her about picking up after herself, she would yell and swear at me.

"You're making a big deal of nothing. Chill out," she would say. "You're too uptight. Stop being such a controlling bitch. Leave me alone," or the conversation stopper, "Fuck off!"

It was easier to clean than to fight. If I said anything, she pounced on my words and would yell at me. I felt trapped and stuck in my own home. I tried to rationalize our situation. We had done everything to support her. I felt that this behavior was the result of a difficult transition period. Bianca was trying to find her way as a legal adult without the structure that the residential treatment facilities had provided during her adolescence. As difficult as her behavior and sloppiness was, I had grown used to this skewed pattern of living. It happened gradually over the summer months and I adapted. She was 18 but acted much younger. Her mental illness kept her off balance and made it difficult to function as an adult. I wasn't excusing her behavior as much as trying to understand the challenges she was facing. I thought that given time, she would settle in and adjust to living at home. My plan was to get her back into counseling and find a psychiatrist who would be able to stabilize her mood with medication. In the meantime, it was important to support her so these goals could be accomplished even if that meant putting up with unpleasant behaviors.

I thought I was misplacing things - nothing alarming or terribly expensive - just some costume jewelry, spare change, a few pictures and knickknacks. I couldn't remember when I saw them last or where I might have left them. I chalked it up to living in a large house, having lots of teenagers coming and going, overall stress, lack of sleep and general forgetfulness. But underneath it all was the nagging thought that Bianca might be responsible for the missing items. We bought a safe to secure the valuables as a precautionary measure and to prevent temptation. I was diligent and kept my wallet in it when I was home. If I forgot to do this, a few dollars would be missing when I went to the store. Bianca denied taking the money, angry that I accused her of stealing.

"I didn't take your money. What are you accusing me for?" she said.

She was furious that I used a safe and peppered her speech with profanity. I did not engage in debate. I repeated clear, unemotional, non-accusatory "I" statements.

"The safe is to secure my wallet and valuables. I choose to keep them there," I told her.

One day while I was at work, the phone rang. Target credit fraud was calling to question if I had authorized $5,000 in purchases at their store in a neighboring town. I was shocked and replied that I did not spend or authorize that activity on my credit card. They immediately froze my account and sent the transaction information. My Target card had been used to buy clothing, pocketbooks, CDs, cell phones and lots of electronics. The date on the receipt was the same day that I had dropped Bianca and a friend off at the mall. This was not a mistake. Bianca stole my Target card and used it without permission. When I confronted her about this, she initially denied everything.

When I explained that I could not afford nor would I pay the bill, she was dismissive and unapologetic.

"So what? It's no big deal," she said.

I explained that since I chose not to pay the bill and that the card was used without my permission and that, in fact, she had stolen it, Target's fraud detection unit was going to investigate. It was out of my hands. I let her know that Target would involve the police and court. She had nothing more to say.

I closed the Target account, drove to the police station, filed a complaint, signed a written statement of the events and submitted the Target transactions. I agreed to work with the police and the Target fraud unit. In doing so, I was released from the responsibility of paying the bill. This authorized Target's credit card fraud division and the police to investigate and bring the case to court.

Because the amount was more than $250 dollars, the complaint automatically became a felony: Theft and unauthorized use of a credit card with intent to commit fraud. I realized that Bianca would be charged and that this would appear on her record permanently, but she had to be held accountable. What she did was wrong. She stole from me, lied and used my card to purchase thousands of dollars in merchandise without permission. She violated my property and in doing so lost my trust. But she did not care.

It got worse. I was missing jewelry and electronics: Earrings, rings, a Tom Tom GPS, radio and karaoke machine. Did I misplace them? Between sleep deprivation and living in chaos, I began to doubt my memory. My Bose radio was gone. Bianca offhandedly mentioned that she had dropped it by accident. She said she was moving it to listen to the music outdoors when it slipped out of her hands and landed on the floor. She took it to be repaired but did not have the repair slip. When questioned further, she replied, "It was broken and the shop said it couldn't be fixed, so I left it there."

She didn't remember the name of the store.

"You had no right to take my radio and bring it to be repaired and leave it there without my permission," I said. She was furious that I was upset.

Once again, she spewed vicious profanity at me and said, "It was only a stupid radio. Get over it."

While I was securing valuables in the house to prevent theft, bags of clothes, accessories and electronics were being delivered to Bianca. Neighbors reported that there were many cars pulling up to the driveway while we were at work during the day. She was suddenly busy with phone calls, sorting through merchandise and meeting cars at the end of the driveway. I saw her carrying packages to and from the house. Her room was strewn with clothes, electronics and cell phones. When I questioned the legality of her activity based on my observations and the neighbors' statements, she exploded. She adamantly denied any wrongdoing and accused me of making things up.

She shouted, "You're the one with the problem, Mom. You are so paranoid. I'm not doing anything wrong. These bags belong to my friends, and I'm holding their things while they look for housing. We trade clothes and stuff. I'm doing them a favor. We are helping each other, and you're the one interfering, trying to make a big deal out of nothing and cause trouble. Get off my back and leave me alone." The profanity she used during these tirades would have shocked even the most hardened criminal.

She was good at turning the tables, giving a logical explanation to my suspicion and then blaming me for questioning her and causing trouble. I started to believe what she was saying and doubt what I was seeing.

One afternoon I received a hysterical call. Bianca called the police because two men were at the house demanding the return of their money for a cell phone they bought, saying that it did not work. I raced home. She was outside. The police were in the driveway; the men were sitting in a car. They explained that Bianca had sold them a cell phone and it did not work. They were returning the cell phone and wanted their money back, not looking for trouble. The situation was finally sorted out and tempers cooled with police presence. She took back the phone and their money was refunded. Everyone was satisfied and the police logged the incident. She was unusually quiet afterward and refused to discuss what happened.

Our local newspaper police log reported the call as a "disagreement between parties about a malfunctioning purchase with peace restored" at our address later that week. Detective Drake from the criminal investigation unit called me to follow up with the police report and to gather more information about Bianca's activities and follow up with the pending Target case. She had already received a summons to appear in court for a hearing the following month. I shared my concerns about her general behavior, missing household items, the broken Bose radio and cell phone incident, all of the driveway activity and Bianca's explanation about the bags of goods in our house. The detective was the first person to mention that she was very likely involved in stealing to support drug use. The missing items, the bags of merchandise and the fraudulent credit card use were common methods that addicts use to pay for drugs. I couldn't believe what I was hearing, but when I thought about the detective's remarks and looked objectively at all of the events put together it made sense.

I confronted Bianca and shared my conversation with the detective as well as our suspicions in light of the facts. She was livid.

The phone rang after supper. A man's voice with a thick accent made it hard to understand his words. I eventually figured out that he was looking for Bianca. He was calling her about a cell phone for sale on Craig's List.

I had heard enough. I ended the conversation abruptly and walked to the television room. She was sitting on the couch with Sam. I asked to speak with her privately.

"I ain't leavin'," she said. "Sam can hear what you have to say."

I asked her what was going on. "Why is this man calling for a cell phone that you are selling on Craig's List?" I said.

I held my ground and didn't back down from the tirade that was about to begin. I was firm and clear as I proceeded to set down rules. The trail of possessions coming into the house would stop, and no one was allowed onto our property unless they were invited and had my prior approval. Sam could not spend the day at our home while we were at work any longer. The stealing would stop, or I would get a restraining order from the courts against her.

Bianca went wild. She stood up from the couch and called me a liar, punctuating her speech once again with vicious profanity.

Suddenly, I lost my temper. I had hit my limit after all the months of putting up with her verbal abuse, flagrant disregard for rules, interrupted sleep, chaos, drama and upheaval in our home. I threw the phone at her.

Bianca leaped over the couch without a moment of hesitation and was standing in front of me before I had a chance to run. There was no way to escape. I stood my ground and tried to remain calm and confident. I was the mother after all and this was my house. Inside, however, I was scared that I was going to get seriously hurt. With raised fists she threatened to beat me up.

"I'm going to smash your face into pulp, you bitch!" she shouted.

Our youngest son stepped in front of her. His quick thinking and decisive action prevented her from hitting me. Sam sat on the couch watching television during the entire event. He never looked up.

I took the next day off from work and went to district court. I filed a "Do Not Harass" order against Bianca. I provided the court evidence from the fraudulent Target card and swore to "tell the truth and nothing but the truth, so help me God."

I couldn't help but notice a few of the court officers snickering when the judge inquired, "So, you want a restraining order against your daughter who is living in your house?"

How could I explain the fear of being afraid and locking valuables in a safe so they wouldn't be stolen, dealing with missing items while living with verbal threats as well as emotional and verbal abuse? Our mentally ill daughter was struggling. She was dependent and unable to live on her own. We were trying to work with her and get her help. I was morally obligated to care for her but had reached my limit. I had to protect myself. That is what I was attempting to do in court. The alternative was to kick her out of the house, and we were not prepared to do that. The judge granted the "Do Not Harass" order against her, and I brought the signed paper home. When I showed it to her and explained what it meant, I expected another outburst. It never came. Bianca was unfazed.

The theft of items and illicit curbside activity immediately stopped. I was not certain it had stopped completely but did not witness any of the usual traffic patterns that had previously plagued our yard. Our personal possessions were intact. In spite of this, our family walked on eggshells, waiting for the next outburst. Sam was a regular presence, but he had managed to find employment over the holidays stocking shelves on the overnight shift. When I came home from work, he was no longer sleeping on the couch, Bianca was better behaved and I was grateful for the respite.

Working full time was tiring enough without being greeted with the remains of their daily activities.

It was still a tenuous arrangement, and the fragile peace in our house could be broken at any moment. She would swear each time I asked that she pick up after herself. It was sometimes easier to just do it myself, and I kept myself safe from her explosions that way. In hindsight, this enabled her to disregard doing her fair share of reasonable chores to keep the household running smoothly. I was extremely unhappy about the negativity of our interactions. I felt helpless to change but hoped that in time and with patience she would improve.

Sam lost his holiday job stocking shelves at Kohl's when the season ended and slowly resumed the habit of being dropped off at our house while we were at work. Once again, I was coming home to a mess after work. Bianca's outbursts and disregard for the impact these behaviors had on the family continued. We insisted that Sam go home each evening by 9 o'clock, and his mother would faithfully come to pick him up at the end of the driveway.

One night the driveway light was triggered, bathing our bedroom in bright shadows. I woke and went to the window. Bianca was walking to the end of the driveway and got into a car, which then drove off. I did not recognize the car, and when I called and texted her she did not answer. I waited. She returned within the hour but refused to tell us where she had been.

"I was with friends," she said.

I was up a lot at night and although the stealing had stopped, the mess and pattern of Bianca and Sam hanging out had resumed. I arrived home to find them passed out on the couch. After waking, they would descend on the kitchen and help themselves to plates of food. They carried their meals down to the finished basement and refused requests to join us at the dinner table. This was a mixed blessing. While I wanted to have a chance for shared mealtime, it was best that she ate elsewhere as the dinner table was a stage for her to showcase her anger. When she did join us, meals were tense. Manners were absent or abhorrent with her feet up on the chair, chewing with her mouth open and talking with food in her mouth along with a lot of swearing and verbal challenges. She would set a trap with an outrageous statement and wait for me to respond. If an alternate choice or opinion was offered, the trap was sprung and the verbal duel would begin. If I did not rise to the baited trap, she would continue to make more outrageous statements. Meals were a battle zone so it was easier and certainly more peaceful to have them eat in the basement.

Sam and Bianca were without income or transportation — two peas in a pod. We rationalized their dependent existence in our house. He was keeping her off the streets and seemed to be a stabilizing influence. I learned later that Sam regularly forced her to have sex with him and other men in exchange for heroin. He was an established heroin addict and pimped our daughter to feed their habit. While we were asleep and Sam was safely tucked into bed at his home, Bianca would leave our house in the middle of the night and meet men at the end of our driveway. She was turning tricks to get money or heroin to share with Sam the following morning. He was always quiet and polite in our home, and I had no indication of the deep darkness that heroin played in their relationship. Had we known that he was pimping our daughter to supply their drug habit, we would have filed a restraining order against him and kicked him off our premises. I should have taken the hint from our dog that he was bad news; Black Jack always growled at him.

By March, Sam had been kicked out of his house. The details surrounding his departure were vague. I concluded that there were ongoing issues that were none of my business, still unaware that he was a heroin addict. His family had given him an intervention, using tough love confrontation to tell him to stop using heroin or leave the house. I had enough to deal with and did not press for further information as it was none of my business. Bianca pleaded for Sam to move in with us, but we were resolute. He could visit for the day, but we had three children already and were not going to be responsible for a fourth dependent living under our roof. We said that he had to be out of the house that evening. He had a choice. We could either bring him to a homeless shelter or drive him back to his parents. The afternoon crept by and dinner came and went. Sam was still in our house. He refused to discuss it with us. Karl and I stood before him and gave him a final ultimatum: "Leave now. We will drive you to the nearest homeless shelter or bring you home. If you refuse to leave, we will call the police to help us remove you from our home as an unwanted guest."

Sam chose to be driven home. After he left, Bianca went on a tirade. She started to throw things, swear and slam furniture. I was accosted in the foyer.

"You people," she spat, using vicious profanity once more.

"I can't believe this. Who do you think you are? I hate you!"

It was a violent outburst, and when she jumped out of the second floor window, we called 911.

The police and ambulance came to our home. They did not use sirens but the flashing red and blue lights shone throughout the neighborhood, interrupting the quiet night. Bianca was sitting in front of the house by the bushes that broke her fall. As she was strapped onto the gurney and loaded into the back of the ambulance, I felt strangely disconnected. We had been through this so many times before that I had lost count. It was terrifying and comforting at the same time. She was desperately ill and was finally getting help. We would be getting a break. Our neighbors, through all of the unwelcome activity on our property, were kind. There were no crowds of onlookers. They gave Bianca her privacy that night, as her illness spilled out into the yard for public display.

Karl and I were accustomed to the police, ambulance and emergency room procedures even though they were stressful and gut wrenching to endure. The staff was professional, kind and understanding. The emergency evaluation concluded that Bianca was not a danger to herself or others.

"I am not going to hurt myself," she said sweetly.

I couldn't help but wonder if she knew the drill, so to speak, and was reluctant to seek help because it involved curbing her lifestyle. She knew just what to say and how to say it. The emergency room staff was just as relieved to send her back to a stable home with family.

I wasn't sure that Bianca was as safe as she proclaimed. I could not say "no" and refuse to bring her home. I could not force her to get help or ask that she be hospitalized for stabilization. She was 19 and legally responsible for herself. She was subsequently discharged home at 1 o'clock in the morning. It had been a long night, and we dragged ourselves to work the next day, running on the fumes of four hours of a restless night's sleep.

As March turned into April, the situation at home did not improve. Her bedroom was a heap of dirty clothes, food, dishes, cosmetics, toiletries and hair accessories strewn about in a careless, tangled, smelly mess. She started to cut and rip her clothes. I hid scissors and sharp knives, afraid of the damage she could inflict on herself or us. We tiptoed around her volatile temper, waiting for the next outburst. Our expectations were fulfilled as they came with regular intensity. Bianca continued unabatedly to pierce herself with sewing needles or safety pins. Her eyebrow, nose, ears, upper and lower lip and navel were adorned with crude and spiky studs. The cuts on her forearms were a landscape of jagged crisscrossing lacerations in various stages of healing. Her arms were in shreds. Her face had six piercings. Her hair color changed every few days from bleached blonde to fluorescent red, orange, green and blue. We never knew what to expect. Hygiene was nonexistent. She did not brush her teeth or bathe.

Things went from bad to worse. My engagement ring that had been soaking in ring cleanser was gone. Also missing were my strand of pearls, silver and our television. Relatives phoned to ask about their lost money and jewelry, as well -

my mother, sister and sister-in-law. Our housecleaner also reported that her cell phone had been stolen from the kitchen counter while she was upstairs cleaning. When confronted with the thefts, Bianca did not accept responsibility or apologize. She denied involvement and all of the items were irretrievable, having been quickly pawned.

One happy event occurred in the midst of all the theft. Sam broke up with her. He swiftly ended their relationship after the housekeeper's cell phone was stolen. I was surprised to learn that the woman was a former neighbor and close friend of Sam's mother. While he accepted money pimped from Bianca, apparently it was too much when she crossed the line and stole from a family friend.

When our eldest son, Michael, came home on military leave from deployment in Turkey, he was worried about the deterioration in his sister's appearance and behaviors while he was away. Michael did not approve of how we handled Bianca. He felt we were too lenient and was upset at her abusive language and disregard for house rules. While I agreed with his assessment, we were actively working to get her back on DMH caseload and had the "Do Not Harass" court order as well as her felony charge in place. The last year had not been successful, and the weight of evidence demonstrated that she needed services. The application was completed, and we were waiting for a "determination of need" finding. In the meantime, we were trying to stabilize her in a safe environment. The alternative was to put her in a homeless shelter or on the streets.

Within a week of the breakup with Sam, she began an all-consuming relationship with a new boyfriend, Mick. Mick lived in Gloucester public housing with his mother and family. He seemed nice enough and was helpful around the house when he came to visit. He mowed the lawn and got along with our youngest son, Stephen. Although he didn't drive, friends dropped him off and the rest of the time he took the commuter rail to our house and walked from the station. I was encouraged that the dog liked him.

While Michael was home on leave, he avoided direct interaction with his sister. He was busy making wedding plans with his fiancée and did not want a confrontation. At the end of his two-week leave, he was packed and ready to report for duty. He was required to contact his commander to get onto the military post upon arrival. We were preparing to get in the car and drive to the airport when he suddenly remembered he had left his cell phone on the kitchen counter to charge while saying goodbye to his fiancée, but he could not find it. We searched the house while the clock was ticking. We had to leave immediately to get to the airport on time. The cell phone was not in the house; it was nowhere to be found. Michael was frantic. We looked everywhere: Between seat cushions, under furniture, in closets, laundry bins and in the trash.

At this time, Bianca and Mick were not in the house. This was curious as they typically "hung out" in the basement. But they were gone and so was Michael's cell phone. I tried to call her. The phone rang once and immediately went to voicemail. She did not call back, nor did she respond to texts. Michael was beside himself. He had no way to contact his commander to return to base in a war zone. All of his pictures, contacts and his life were in his cell phone. I don't know how I managed to get him calmed down and on the scheduled flight, but I gave him my cell phone to take with him. It did not have international service, but at least it worked and he had a phone. It was a heartbreaking goodbye as he walked away from the car. I was sick with the worry of him going back into a combat zone with no way to contact his commander.

At that moment I realized that I had reached the end of my patience with Bianca. She had crossed the line and put Michael in danger. I would no longer tolerate her abuse of me, our family, our house, belongings or our emotions. I was done. She was no longer welcome in our home. I called Karl and he agreed. Next, I called the locksmith and had all the locks on the house changed within the hour. I left her a voice message: "Do not come home," I said. "You are not welcome here. You do not live here anymore."

chapter **5**

INTO THE INFERNO

Bianca spent the summer sleeping in the park in Gloucester and couch surfing with acquaintances. Occasionally, she would stay at the home her new boyfriend, Mick. We talked to Mick's mother, and she agreed to let Bianca stay there but needed some financial support for room and board. I was happy to supplement this arrangement, as it kept her off the streets and they were gracious to accommodate her. But by the end of the summer, Bianca was evicted from Mick's house. She made threats against his former girlfriend, the mother of his child, and the family filed a restraining order against her. She stayed with Mick's aunt for a few weeks, but that arrangement was temporary and ended abruptly. She was living on the streets once more, sleeping in the homeless shelter some nights and in the park on nights that were warm.

She used church meals and shelter services to get by.

Karl would meet Bianca and bring her bags of ready-to-eat food and warm clothes. I accompanied him on a few of these trips but did not communicate directly with her during this time. She continued to make threats against individuals with whom she had conflict, and there were additional restraining orders filed against her. I kept a safe distance from her and did not see her alone.

As autumn approached, the nights got colder and street living became more difficult. On nights that were below freezing and if the shelters were full, she would call, crying and frantic. We would drive to Gloucester and pick up Bianca and Mick. I held firm and did not allow her to return home. It was hard to watch her try to live on the streets, but I decided that my priority was to protect myself from her abuse. We begged her to get help but our requests fell on deaf ears. She broke promises repeatedly, and her words meant nothing. She was not making attempts to get better or improve her situation. We would help her as much as we could, but she would not live under our roof again. Tough love was not an easy road to travel, but it was absolutely necessary.

On more than one occasion, we drove for several hours looking for inexpensive motels for Bianca and Mick to stay in overnight. I usually went to the front desk to inquire about room vacancies. She stayed in several motels along Route 1, and we tried to reserve as many nights as possible. Each one lasted until she was asked to leave because she stole clothes from dryers and threatened guests.

In the meantime, Karl was in contact with an acquaintance

that had an apartment for rent in Gloucester. We helped Bianca move on a bitterly cold day. The wind was howling with gale force, driving the temperature well below freezing and she was pleased and grateful for this warm space. We gave her some furniture and surplus dishes, and she took her bed and a bureau from home. The apartment was downtown, simply furnished, clean and safe. We all breathed a sigh of relief and were thankful that the living situation was settled and she was off the streets before snowfall.

The apartment was a stabilizing force through the winter. Bianca settled down and was a regular presence during the day at the local shelter. She had connected with DMH and received food bank supplements. She also used her food stamps to buy and cook her food. Last, but certainly not least, she began GED tutoring and worked with shelter staff to locate part-time employment. There were no further outbursts or court appearances.

When she came home for a visit at Christmas, Michael's deployment was over and it was the first holiday that our family was together in several years. Michael and Bianca avoided being in the house at the same time, but she did apologize to him for stealing his cell phone. He was unable to let go of her betrayal, however, and the loss of his information and pictures. Their reconciliation was incomplete and never fully recovered.

With the arrival of spring, Bianca's behaviors escalated again. Warm weather, long days and blooming trees had a negative effect on her mood. She became increasingly angry, hostile, paranoid and explosive, which manifested in swearing, cutting, disrupted sleep, appetite fluctuations, poor hygiene, door slamming, object throwing and stomping. We braced ourselves.

Mick called the house after midnight to let us know that Bianca was in the emergency room. She had suffered a seizure at the apartment and he called 911. She was stable and would be released soon. He just wanted us to know that she was safe and okay. I was worried about the seizure as she had never had one before. Mick reassured us that the doctors were satisfied that she was well enough to be released. She had a follow-up appointment with her doctor at the public health clinic the following day, and when we saw her she looked pale and tired. She said that she didn't know what happened. We never did learn what caused the seizure. I wondered if she had overdosed and thought that she and Mick were not telling the entire truth of the situation.

In May, Bianca was evicted from the apartment. There were too many complaints from the neighbors about noise and the number of people coming and going at all hours. When we went to help her move out of the apartment, I gagged. The place was infested. The filth in the bathroom and kitchen was thick, black and crawling with fleas. They were everywhere. The plumbing overflowed from a clogged garbage disposal and dishwasher drain. There was trash, old food and unwiped spills all over. The walls were smeared with fingerprints and food. The carpet and floors were thick with grime. The pretty apartment had turned into a flop house in the span of six months. We paid to have it professionally cleaned and the damages repaired. The exterminator said that it was the worst case of fleas he had ever seen in his 35 years in the industry.

Bianca was arrested several times in the cities of Gloucester, Salem and Quincy over the span of eight weeks. The charges were varied and included stealing a neighbor's puppy, violating several restraining orders taken out against her by Mick's family, solicitation, possession of heroin and trespassing. The complaints included physical aggression and threats of violence, disturbing the peace, dealing drugs, selling stolen property and panhandling on Boston Common. Bianca broke up with Mick as a direct result of her threats of violence against his family as well as the arrests and her overall bad influence. His family moved him away from Bianca, settled him in another town and got him into counseling and alcohol and drug treatment. I was hopeful that he would get well with these interventions, but I never learned how he fared. We didn't see or hear from him again.

Bianca was arrested when she tried to hawk a stolen cell phone. One of her friends had stolen it with her help. The phone was taken from a high school student, and her parents reported it missing to police. A covert "sting" operation was set up, and when she arrived to exchange the "hot" phone for money she was arrested. She spent the night in jail and appeared in court the following day. I took the day off from work to attend the arraignment and posted bail. She was assigned a probation officer and mandated counseling through DMH. Bianca agreed to the terms, and I was hopeful again that the additional oversight by the court would curb her illegal activity.

We were trying to find another place for her to live. She refused in-patient hospitalization and did not show up at counseling appointments. She also avoided responsibility most of the time, although she did walk to the court to meet with her probation officer once.

"There's nothin' wrong with me," she said. "You ain't lockin' me up." Once again, she made liberal use of profanity when speaking.

In the meantime, she was couch surfing in friends' and acquaintances' apartments. We were powerless to convince her that she needed to get help. We opened statements from Blue Cross for medical care that she received for strep throat, abdominal pain and urinary tract infections from hospitals in Salem and Boston. Bianca was on our insurance plan but because of HIPPA regulations, we were not privy to information about the health care she received. DMH and Medicaid applications were finally approved, much to my relief, because the bills to take care of Bianca and her problems were mounting.

I never knew exactly where she was at any given time, but she did respond to texts and reassured us that she was "doin' okay."

She told us she was looking for work and that she had met with her DMH counselor, but her words were lies. The counselors were in contact with Karl, informing him that she continued to miss appointments. She was not following the terms of her probation and was risking arrest. One afternoon, we got a desperate call to come and get her from the police station. She had been arrested for violating a restraining order. When Karl and I went to the jail to post bail, the police informed us that they saw track marks on her arms. I suspected that she was drinking, smoking marijuana and popping pills, but this was the first hard evidence, poof that she was injecting drugs. The police officer recommended that we involuntarily commit Bianca to get her off the streets and into drug rehabilitation. We thought this would be a good solution, but she was not crazy enough to commit involuntarily. She denied that she was injecting drugs.

We tried to get her to agree to in-patient addiction treatment or outpatient counseling but she adamantly refused.

She was living on the streets again, homeless and couch surfing overnight at the homes of friends. On occasion, she would spend a night or two in a shelter if the weather was bad or she had nowhere else to sleep. She texted regularly, asking for money and food and we would arrange to meet and bring groceries, money and clothes. I did not meet or go with her alone. My personal possessions were secure, and my cell phone was pre-dialed to place an emergency call if needed. Her behavior, although erratic, was not violent but I was taking no chances. She was usually with a friend and happily made introductions. She never complained about her situation or asked to come home. I felt guilty that she was homeless but determined that she could not live with us again until she found a steady job, agreed to counseling and stopped getting into trouble with the police. I was still trying to reconcile the fact that she might be injecting drugs. I didn't want to believe it. Each time we met I was relieved that she was safe but worried about her situation and drug use.

Bianca was arrested again on a Friday night headed into a long 4th of July weekend. The phone rang at dinner. The call was from the Gloucester police station. I immediately picked up the phone, dreading what I would hear. She was calling with a desperate plea for us to post bail. We did not have the cash on hand and were not willing to go to the ATM to get it so we refused. I was tired of her behavior and empty promises. I was tired of the phone calls at all hours of the night. I was tired of the endless drama. I was tired of her lies, the abuse, the stealing, the arrests, posting bail and bringing her to court. I was exhausted from the countless trips to the emergency room, the hospitalizations and all of the complaints. Most of all, I was tired of mental illness and her addiction. I loved her but loved myself more. I couldn't do it any longer. For the first time we refused to help. We simply said, "No, we cannot bail you out."

The police called us later that evening. After our phone conversation, Bianca threatened to commit suicide in the holding cell. Instead of going to MCI Framingham for lock-up, she was transported to Tewksbury State Hospital where she was admitted. She was going to be held there over the weekend until her arraignment the following Tuesday. We drove to Tewksbury State Hospital on Sunday afternoon, and I brought her a few toiletries and some clean clothes for her court appearance. She was clean, freshly shampooed and showered, sober and quiet when we saw her. She was afraid of staying in a psychiatric hospital and felt trapped. She wanted the charges to go away and didn't want any more trouble.

"I did some dumb-ass things and messed up," she admitted. "I want to make it right and get out of here. People are crazy in this place."

The court-appointed attorneys in both Salem and Gloucester

District Courts tried to prevent Bianca from serving time in jail and entered a "not guilty" plea. At her arraignment, we posted bail and she was released on probation with conditions that included staying out of trouble, frequent drug screens, DMH counseling and oversight, as well as regular meetings with her probation officer. Her court hearing was scheduled in August. She had two months to stay out of trouble.

We had been looking for an apartment as soon as she left Gloucester. Fortunately, a local landlord had an unexpected vacancy in an apartment in town. Since we were responsible for the lease and we knew the owners of the building, they overlooked her less than desirable tenant traits as a favor. The apartment was on the second floor and had a large sunny kitchen, spacious living room and bedroom complete with a walk-in closet, dishwasher and balcony. There was an added, hidden benefit as well. The apartment building was located next to the police station. The staircase and balcony overlooked the station, and I thought that the close proximity would be a good deterrent to bad behavior. Bianca happily settled into the apartment and kept a low profile, staying out of trouble. Driving by her apartment on my way home after work, I would usually see her sitting on the front steps smoking a cigarette or walking along Main Street. She always smiled and waved at me. When I pulled the car up to the curb to say hello, she would run to where I was parked, and we would chat for a minute or two.

Bianca wasn't alone long. She soon met Rex and he became her new boyfriend and quickly moved in with her. Rex was on probation. He had been released from jail after serving time on a domestic assault and battery sentence. Rex was pleased to meet me. He was clean shaven and neatly dressed.

He spoke well, made eye contact and had a sincere charm. The dog liked him, too. I was glad that Bianca was doing well on probation, and Rex seemed to be a good influence on her. The apartment was neat, clean and well stocked with nutritious food. She was happy and staying out of trouble, clean and sober and looked good each time I saw her. Rex was a licensed barber and was quickly hired at a barbershop on Main Street. She landed a job working the counter at a local coffee shop. Both positions were within walking distance of the apartment and meant steady incomes and a regular schedule. Meanwhile, Bianca was meeting with her DMH counselor and probation officer. Her random drug screens were clean. She was beginning to stabilize.

But the stabilization did not last. Within a month, she and Rex had a fight. It spilled into the street, and the police immediately intervened since it was in front of the station. Rex was arrested for violating the terms of his probation and charged with domestic assault and battery. She fluctuated between being furious at Rex for choking and burning her chest with a cigarette and crying that she loved him and missed him terribly. She was sorry that he was in jail and wanted him back. She was mad that the police arrested him, and in the next breath was glad that he was in jail.

My head was spinning. I was angry that Bianca had been assaulted by her boyfriend. Her professed love for him made no sense to me. I tried to stay calm and keep out of her drama and simply said that it was wrong for anyone to hit or abuse anyone else. The laws were there for her protection and everyone else's. I reminded her that Rex was in jail because he had broken the conditions of his probation. Bianca was not comforted by my words. She was distraught that Rex was behind bars. She wanted to visit him, but this was not allowed because she had an open court case. She was afraid to stay alone in her apartment. In order to manage this fear, she entertained several other boyfriends while Rex was in jail. He invariably found out about these alliances and was not pleased. We rejected phone calls from him while he was in jail. I wanted to stay out of their relationship and in the meantime, I hoped that she would behave herself until her court hearing in August.

But Bianca failed to appear in court on the appointed date in August, and a summons was issued for her arrest. She was later found on the streets, arrested and subsequently brought before the court. She had multiple open cases pending in Quincy, Gloucester, Salem and Beverly.

Upon realizing the number and extent of all of the charges against her, the judge said, "Young lady, your past has caught up with you."

She pled guilty to all of the charges rather than continue with probation and drug screens. She wanted her cases to go away. The only way for this to happen would be to plead guilty and serve time, even if it meant that she would have a criminal record. Bianca received an eight-month jail sentence and was promptly sent to MCI Framingham with a release date in March. We terminated the apartment lease and emptied her apartment, bringing her belongings to our basement for storage.

With Bianca off the streets, we slept better at night. We arranged for her to make collect telephone calls to us from jail. Karl spent one weekend day each month traveling to the women's state prison in Framingham. He would be gone the better part of a day for the brief 50-minute visit with her. It was a relief to have her contained but heartbreaking to realize that our daughter was a convicted felon because of her addiction-driven mental illness. Society determined that she had to be punished for her misdeeds, and we knew this was necessary even though it broke our hearts.

After several months of good inmate behavior, she was moved to a community-based incarceration setting in Salisbury, Massachusetts. It was still a secure correctional facility, but the inmates were living in a more open, dorm-like environment. The rooms could be locked, but there were no bars on the doors or windows. Guard surveillance was constant and the rules were strict. We no longer had to be bodily searched in order to visit. We still had to show identification, and packages were inspected. We could not bring homemade food into the setting. It had to come from a store and be wrapped in the original container. We brought clothes, shoes, toiletries, school supplies and bedding. Bianca was given community service passes with correctional officer oversight, as well as the opportunity to work at a local motel cleaning units as a chambermaid. She received much needed services while she was incarcerated, which included psychiatric and substance abuse counseling, high school equivalency test preparations and vocational training. It was a good fit. During our family visit at Thanksgiving, she was in good spirits and proud that she was serving the remainder of her time there for good behavior. We brought Dunkin' Donuts hot chocolate and coffees to share in the common lounge during our visits.

On our next trip, we were alarmed to discover that Bianca

was not at the Salisbury site. The officer in charge said that she was back at the state prison. He would not provide details and tell us what happened, but we did get permission to collect her belongings.

The following weekend we went to MCI Framingham. Bianca told us that she was kicked out of the program for bringing drugs (cocaine) into the halfway house. She "found" it in one of the rooms in the motel she was cleaning. She insisted that it was all a big misunderstanding. She did not intend to break the rules or use the drugs. She simply found them and was "holding" them for a friend as a favor. The drugs were discovered during routine patrol, and they were sniffed out by a guard dog. She was promptly removed from the halfway house and returned to the women's state prison where she would serve the remaining three months of her eight-month sentence. She lasted eight weeks in the halfway house before a bad decision caught up with her.

MCI Framingham continued to offer drug counseling, Narcotics Anonymous (NA) and Alcoholics Anonymous (AA) group therapy as well as GED tutoring, job counseling and level entry work training in areas such as food preparation, hair styling and manicures. Bianca worked on her GED study plan and regularly attended AA and NA classes. She wrote in her journal about the dangers of drugs and her relief to finally be drug free. She liked working in the nail salon and planned to pursue this as a career upon release. The time in jail was well spent. Bianca was clean and sober and proud of her accomplishments. She was looking forward to her future. I was hopeful that this experience would turn her life around and be a new beginning for her and us.

As her release from jail approached, we were able to connect with DMH who, in turn, contacted the MCI Framingham social worker/counselor. DMH determined that Bianca qualified to be discharged from jail directly into a transition house in Peabody, Massachusetts, and a bed was located and secured. DMH had also arranged wraparound services, including counseling, adult day center to help with medication management, career coaching and GED preparation in addition to safe housing in Peabody. Everything was finalized and in place before her release. When discharge day arrived, she was given a pair of new sneakers along with $50 and a ride to the train station.

Karl met Bianca at the depot and drove her to the transition house. She was proud to be clean and sober and outlined her plans to work with DMH, but within one week she was having trouble. She did not follow curfews and came in late or did not return until the morning. After multiple offenses, she was asked to leave. We didn't know what to do or how to help. I was terrified that she would be on the streets again and tempted to use drugs without some form of oversight. DMH recommended a local, inexpensive hotel in Chelsea that had rooms for rent. Fortunately, there was a vacancy at the hotel and we paid the week's rent in advance. She was off the streets and within walking distance of DMH headquarters where she could attend counseling, GED classes and drop into a lounge there. She was happy to be out of Peabody and confided that male clients were hitting on her, and she didn't want to stay there. She liked her room at the hotel.

Meanwhile, Rex was released from jail, and his sentence was suspended for good behavior. I was uneasy about the restoration of their relationship, given the assault on Bianca the previous year. We watched helplessly as he moved in with her at the hotel. As the summer progressed, we received calls that she was disturbing the peace in the hotel and had stolen women's clothes from the laundromat. The owner told us that she was hanging around with a bad crowd. The hotel had a reputation for housing troubled individuals, and there were regular entries in the local newspaper highlighting various assaults, drug deals and arrests. It must have taken a lot of bad behavior for her to rise to this level of notoriety in that building. She was warned that if she gave them any more trouble, she would be evicted from the hotel.

Later that spring, Bianca called at 1 o'clock in the morning, hysterical. Rex had beaten her. The noise alerted hotel staff and the police were called. He was arrested, having violated the conditions of his probation. The following morning, he was returned to jail to serve the remainder of his term. Shortly after, she was issued a summons to appear in court to face the charge of perjury. The jail taped a conversation between her and Rex. In the tape, she was heard to say that she would lie in court and tell the judge that he did not hit her. This was in direct opposition to the statement she made to the police on the night Rex assaulted her and was arrested. She went to court on the summons and was appointed an attorney. The attorney then argued that given her mental illness and involvement with DMH, she was a victim rather than a perpetrator. The judge agreed. She was released and a hearing was scheduled in one month. Meanwhile, she met with her attorney who emphasized the need to be truthful, leave the abusive relationship and use the resources available to her. Bianca agreed that it was wrong for Rex to hit her; however, it did little to deter her infatuation with this man. "I still love him," she said.

I could only watch and hope that she would come to her senses and leave him before something worse happened.

Bianca was eventually asked to leave the hotel and stayed with various friends. This was a volatile and temporary arrangement until housing could be secured. The people she hung around with had their own issues and varying degrees of instability, past incarcerations, psychiatric hospitalizations and substance use. Her association with them caused a lot of drama and misunderstandings, which ultimately spilled over into our lives. She stopped by our house on the 4th of July in the midst of a fight with her friends. Our guests witnessed our daughter in action firsthand. It was typical behavior when her bipolar disease was escalating under the influence. She was manic. Her words were fast and so pressured that I could barely understand what she was saying. She was arguing on her cell phone and swearing at her friends. I am not sure what the disagreement was about, but her appearance and yelling were alarming. The friends she was fighting with eventually picked her up in front of the house, and they left to see fireworks. Our evening was ruined.

Within one week, Bianca had a witnessed drug overdose. She "dropped" in the street after injecting heroin and a passerby called 911. The emergency room doctor administered six doses of naloxone to reverse her overdose and staff rubbed her chest raw to keep her awake and breathing. When she was discharged the following morning, she was given papers containing a list of support groups, social services and counselors. We never knew this happened because the emergency room did not notify us. We only learned about this a few days later when we saw her. She gave us some information but only a little of what she remembered, which wasn't very much. We learned a few more details of her overdose when we opened an itemized bill for hospital services the following month.

Bianca was truly remorseful after this overdose. We had a heart-to-heart conversation, and I told her that I loved her and would help her but first she had to help herself. She couldn't continue the way she had been living. She said that she wanted to stay off drugs and that what happened had frightened her. She was also ashamed of her situation: The arrests, the court cases and the overdose. She agreed to talk with DMH counselors, attend support groups, follow up with her primary care doctor and work with Massachusetts Rehabilitation to find a job. She gave me a hug and said, "Thank you, Mommy, for never calling me a junkie. I love you to the moon and back. I am ready to kick this. I will do it. I promise."

It was a sweet moment. Bianca was sincere in her promise to lead a happy, clean and sober life. She spoke from her heart in the midst of chaos and wanted to be well. I promised to always love her even if that meant setting limits and holding her accountable. I remember every detail of our conversation, and for the first time in many years I was hopeful that her promise was real.

Since her eviction from the hotel, we were again, for the third time, able to secure housing. She was set up in a sweet apartment that was quiet, private and on the first floor next to a park in town. She was happy there and was meeting with her DMH counselors. But then, we were shocked to get a telephone call from the western part of Massachusetts in the middle of the night one week later.

"I am in Springfield with three men," she said. "Can you come and get me?"

It was too far and too late, and we were in no condition to travel 120 miles in the middle of the night to get her. I was half asleep. She was with a female friend, and we advised her to stay with the woman and call the police if needed. She texted the following morning to say that she was home safe. I looked on her Facebook page and was shocked to see pictures of her dressed up for a night on the town. We barely recognized our daughter, and I did not recognize the other women in the picture. I couldn't believe what I was seeing and tried to wrap my head around the fact that she was involved in prostitution. Once more, I was helpless to stop her. Our beautiful Bianca was deteriorating before my eyes.

DMH counselors were not able to meet with her. She failed to show up at pre-arranged appointments, and she did not return phone calls. I arranged a primary care doctor appointment, as she had been without a medical provider since leaving the group home at age 18. This was a prerequisite first step in order to connect with a psychiatrist. She wasn't home when Karl went to pick her up. He had taken a day off from work and was frustrated that she blew off the appointment. We issued an ultimatum. If she didn't attend meetings and participate in her plan, then we would cut her off from our financial support. Without her active participation in the recovery plan, she would not succeed getting clean and staying sober.

"You need this to live," we told her.

The challenge worked and she did agree to the terms. The counselors said, "We don't know what you did, but she is answering our calls and attending her appointments." We were encouraged and hopeful once more that this would be the time she would finally succeed and keep her promise.

The following weekend was our annual city-wide homecoming event. Bianca and her brother came over for a cookout. We grilled burgers and ate on the porch because she refused to come in contact with any insects in the backyard. We laughed a lot that day. She was in good spirits, made jokes and poked fun at us all. After dinner, I got out the hula-hoop and we took turns trying to coordinate our movements to keep the ring aloft in time with hip-hop music blaring from the stereo. It was hilarious and one of the funniest moments we had shared together in a long time. When it was time to go, she gave me a big hug.

"I love you to the moon and back, Mommy," she said. She was warm, soft and her skin had the familiar sweet smell that I loved so much. I remember every detail of that precious moment. It was the last time I would ever see, speak with or touch my daughter while alive. She died from a heroin overdose the next day.

EPILOGUE

The sun was already below the horizon when we sat down to eat dinner on Monday, August 10, 2015. The day had been brutally hot and humid with dangerous temperature and air quality warnings. A gentle ocean breeze was starting to bring relief, and I was looking forward to a cooler evening. It felt good to sit down and enjoy a quiet meal. I had been up before sunrise to catch the first train into Boston and begin work promptly at 7 o'clock.

As we talked about our day over dinner, Karl relayed the events from the previous night. He did not want me to worry and be distracted at work, so he waited until now to disclose what had happened. He did not sleep the night before. Bianca had repeatedly called his cell phone and the house phone throughout the night, oblivious to the intrusion on sleep.

"Someone took my phone. I need a new one now!" she

yelled into the phone, making liberal use of profanity.

Reasoning with her was impossible for Karl, and the conversation that night was futile. She demanded that her phone be replaced immediately. When he told her that he could not help her because it was the middle of the night, she swore and hung up, only to call back later. This was typical Bianca behavior: Interrupt our peace and quiet with a crisis demanding immediate resolution and curse and hang up if she didn't get her way or hear what she wanted to hear. After several more outbursts, Karl turned off his phone and did not answer any more of her calls that night. He waited until dinner the following evening to tell me what happened. He didn't want me to lose sleep and go to work tired. We agreed that he would call Bianca the next day, given the late hour. We were too tired and did not have the energy to engage with her that night. He would arrange a convenient time to replace the phone. I was upset that she had bothered her father throughout the night and was relieved that he would deal with her.

The next morning, he was unable to reach Bianca; calls immediately went to her voicemail. He checked her Facebook page and cell phone log and, seeing no activity since Monday morning, he decided to stop by her apartment on the way to work. Arriving there, he called out her name and knocked loudly on the door. There was no response. Everything was quiet inside. He thought that perhaps she was asleep or not at home. He decided to check further and peered through a window to make sure everything was in order. It was then that he saw her feet on the floor of her bedroom. He banged the door again and yelled her name. Her feet did not move. Using the spare key on his keychain, he unlocked the apartment door and went inside. Bianca was on the floor in her bedroom. She did not move when he called her name and touched her. With rising dread, he touched her skin. It was cold and when he checked for a pulse, there was none.

Bianca Lynn Wilson was dead from a drug overdose. She died alone on the floor in her bedroom. The needle, spoon, lighter and heroin were on the nightstand. Our beautiful 21-year-old daughter was gone. We would never see, hear, touch or talk to her again. The years spent living with her promises to get help and stop using heroin were over. There are no words to describe the agony of losing a child. There is no greater pain, and there are no words to comfort. Our hearts are broken.

We tried, but whatever we did just wasn't enough. Bianca had every resource imaginable, all within her grasp and given freely without asking. We promised to help her get well and worked tirelessly. We never gave up. She was given safe housing, a loving family, financial support, rides, groceries, medical care and psychiatric services. We had exhausted ourselves, always hoping that this time she would commit to her treatments, show up for meetings and follow through with the plan. I pleaded with her to stay connected with us and everyone trying to help her. I prayed that she would keep her promises, be accountable and get well.

We constantly told her how much we loved her, how valuable, how precious and how unique she was. We set limits when needed and tried to do all the right things. We supported flute lessons, synchronized swimming, soccer, ballet and Girl Scouts. Karl and I were scout leaders, room mother, coaches and Sunday school teachers. We brought Bianca and her brothers to church every Sunday where she was loved and accepted. We celebrated accomplishments and holidays with friends and extended family. We created a safe, loving family and tirelessly advocated for her by obtaining resources. We never gave up or stopped helping our daughter.

Bianca did not believe our promises. She did not believe that she was worthy of love because she did not have the ability to love herself first. The scores of people and the loving actions of everyone trying to help her get well did not make a difference in the end. She was running from mental illness fueled by the seductive, ferocious grip of heroin. It soothed her pain and filled her emptiness, first with the promise of sweet relief and then with the unrelenting demand to be fed. Bianca hawked my jewelry, stole our property and sold herself to buy drugs.

She emotionally and verbally abused me, our family, her friends and those who were trying to help. She committed fraud, larceny and perjury. She intimidated witnesses, violated restraining orders, was evicted, arrested and incarcerated. She prostituted herself to buy a fix and left chaos in her wake. We watched our beautiful daughter self-destruct in front of our eyes, powerless to do anything. She was living a nightmare and we were helpless to stop it. Nothing we did or could have done differently prevented the overdose. Death started the moment heroin entered her veins, but she lost herself to mental illness many years before.

Why she didn't accept help is a question that will never

be answered. The police were at her door the night she overdosed. There was a 911 call placed from her residence. When the EMTs arrived, the house was dark and quiet. Our daughter lay dying on the other side of the door. Could she have whispered, "Help me" and would they have heard? Would it have saved her life? Would it have made a difference in the final outcome? How long would it last until the next overdose? After each one, we prayed that she would get help, keep her promise to stay clean and stop using drugs. Perhaps it required too much energy. Perhaps the demons were too deep. Perhaps she thought she could get sober tomorrow and have one more heroin-laced day, numb and worry free from mental illness and pain.

We will never know the answers to the remaining questions about Bianca's mental illness and addiction. There are no more chances. There are no more appointments, counselors or detoxification programs that will help. Death, the final act and the aftermath of senseless loss, a life cut short, the potential wasted and the cost of suffering is immeasurable. In spite of everything we did and the scores of people trained to help along with the love of friends and family, it wasn't enough.

Where do we go from here, and how do we move forward? I do not have the answers, but I am thankful for the time we did have with Bianca. It is what keeps me grounded and sane. There are many wonderful and happy memories. I remember how much Bianca enjoyed the beauty and grace of ballet classes, gymnastics and synchronized swimming. Her athleticism was breathtaking to watch. The time spent together during practice and competition was so much fun.

We joked that Bianca was one of the first girls to join the Boy Scout program. Karl and I were Cub Scout leaders and Bianca accompanied her brothers to den and pack meetings. She participated in scouting events, and could out run all of the boys because she was so fast and strong. Family camping trips and yearly vacations were some of our best times together. The daily rhythms of family life kept us active, whether it was swimming in our pool, riding bicycles, going to the beach, building snow men, sledding, or playing in the yard. Fearless, and with a zest for life, Bianca lived with abandon and joy. These are the memories that sustain us.

Did we do enough for Bianca? I do not know. Bianca's death feels like a failure, even though we tried our best, given the resources and strength at the time but it wasn't enough. It would be convenient and easy to blame others for her overdose. Perhaps it would make the grief and guilt easier to bear. Bianca was more than just a mentally ill addict, she was our child and we loved her. I always will. Bianca was kind, thoughtful, exuberant and full of life until mental illness and drugs stole her from us.

If given the choice, would we do it over again? Would we adopt her and suffer through the trauma of those difficult years once more? The answer is yes. We would do it over again. It was worth all of the struggle and pain because our love for Bianca - even in those terrible moments. We loved her through it all, never giving up hope that she would recover from her addiction.

I am thankful for the time that I did have with Bianca and grateful for the many blessings in my life. I treasure the memories of Bianca and our years together, remembering both the good times and the bad. When grief becomes more than I can bear, my faith carries me. The death of our daughter and the years of living with her mental illness and addiction will not cause me to become bitter or angry. I will not let grief interfere with living and hold me prisoner to the past.

My heart breaks each time I read another obituary in the avalanche of opioid overdoses sweeping our nation. These deaths cause overwhelming pain and misery for so many families. Addiction claims the life of its victims, and loved ones are often left to cope with limited resources and support. Feelings of guilt, shame, grief and loss are overwhelming, but they do become more manageable over time. It is my sincere wish that sharing Bianca's story, will reassure families that you can survive illness, addiction and overdose, even when it seems impossible. You are not alone. Mental illness and addiction will never win against the promises of hope and love.

INTERVIEW
with the author

Q: First of all, thank you for writing this book. It's going to help a lot of people understand what drug addiction and its tragic results is all about. Can you tell us how you came to the decision to write the book?

A: When Bianca died, I was adrift for a long time. I was unable to get my bearings, the grief was so deep. I needed to get my feelings out to deal with her death. So, while riding the commuter rail to work, I started to write. It was a way to process all that happened. By writing everything down, I didn't have to carry it anymore. At the time, I had no intention of writing a book.

Q: How did that help you?

A: At first, it didn't help me very much because I was just trying to get it all out. After awhile, I realized that I was telling a story of Bianca's life. It became, at that point, more of a chronicle of what happened to her. I thought that it was important to tell her story because of everything that we had endured. Once I realized that, I said, "Oh, I think there's the making of a book here."

Q: It must have been tremendously difficult for you to rehash everything that happened in such detail.

A: Yes, it was very difficult. There were times when I stopped writing because it was so painful, and the memories threatened to engulf me. I had to brace myself for what was coming next in the story. I was afraid to relive those bad events and reopen old wounds.

Q: The book is a very honest, raw, unpolished look at what it's like to be within this storm of addiction with someone you love. The reality is not pretty and actually does not paint a very positive picture of the person with an addiction. Even so, what can you tell us about Bianca before the addiction?

A: When we adopted Bianca, she was two years old. We enjoyed 10 happy years with her before mental illness began. There were little things along the way that were harbingers of what was to come, but she was kind and loving. I remember her boundless energy and enthusiasm.

Q: Are there any particular memories you could share for her first 10 years?

A: Yes, one stands out in my mind. We took her to our timeshare and we brought her to the pool. She was two-and-a-half years old. I was in the water and we had a bubble on her. I was going to take her hand and bring her into the water and she stood on the edge of the pool and said, "No, I'll do it myself," and she jumped in and she proceeded to swim and she was fearless. She was also very beautiful in the water and years later excelled at synchronized swimming. She was involved in that sport for just under four years and was beautiful and graceful and lovely in the water. She could also outrun any boy in the neighborhood. She was fast, very strong and she never got sick. She would climb the highest tree or stand on the railing on the dock and jump. She was simply fearless.

Q: What else can you share?

A: I think in addition to those qualities, she was very kind. She loved her family and she loved her grandparents, her father and her brothers. She could be very generous and would give things to others when she observed they had little. I think she noticed other children who struggled, and when she was little she was never mean to those children. She would try to go out of her way to play with them. But because she was so exuberant, sometimes on the edge of being out of control in the classroom and on the playground, other mothers didn't always appreciate her exuberance, shall we say, and that could be difficult. There was a time when she didn't get invited to many birthday parties in the neighborhood, and that was hard for her and for me.

Q: The book at times is a difficult read. During her addiction, was it all bad? Can you share with us positive moments even in the throes of difficulties with Bianca?

A: There were some good times in the throes of the bad years, as I call them, when mental illness was raging and she was riding it. I'm trying to remember some specifics; I'm sure they were there. They were just hard to appreciate at the time. I think she was always kind to her brothers even when she was struggling and even when she was so angry at me. She never turned on them and she was always protective with them. She loved her Nana. She was kind to and loved our cat; she loved our dog, and our friends and her babysitters. In spite of the horrible effects of mental illness on her, underneath it she was a kind and loving person.

Q: Were there two Bianca's?

A: Yes. There was the raging mentally ill Bianca. She suffered from bipolar disorder. When she was manic, she could be a good, happy, crazy, funny manic or she could be a wild, crazy, angry, mentally ill bipolar Bianca.

Q: How do you think Bianca saw herself?

A: I think she saw herself as having to struggle a lot because she was adopted. She came to us at the age of two. She had been in a very chaotic, neglectful environment and I think her first two years of self-identity were scarred because of that. When she was growing, she was looking for who she was and it was hard for her. I don't think she saw herself in later years as being lovable, loved and valued.

Q: When did you start to realize that you were dealing with a different person almost, that you weren't dealing with your sweet, kind child but you were dealing with someone else?

A: It came on rather abruptly around the time of puberty and middle school and it wasn't a gradual thing. All of a sudden, literally one day, it was like a switch had flipped and she became extremely difficult, volatile, angry and impossible to deal with in a rational way.

Q: How old was she then?

A: She was 12-and-a-half. Just after her first semester in sixth grade things really started to happen, and there was no wondering what I was seeing or wondering if she was well or not. She was not well and we knew it pretty quickly.

Q: It must be difficult for a parent or a family member of someone with an addiction to distinguish between the two people, if I might say. How difficult is it for a parent to look at an addicted child realistically? With your last comment, you said you pretty much knew right off the bat, there was no question, but some counselors state that an addicted child is not the same person they were before the addiction. What are your thoughts?

A: Well, I didn't realize Bianca was addicted until I had strong evidence, objective evidence. That was probably several years into her addiction. The mental illness...

Q: So, it took a couple of years for you...

A: It did.

Q: ...to accept the reality of the circumstances?

A: The addiction, yes. The mental illness started before her addiction. The mental illness, we knew right away. We knew what we were dealing with, and we tried to get resources for her. I thought that the addiction was just another manifestation of mental illness and trying to be 18 and navigate the world of young adulthood without the structure of group homes and counselors.

I missed the signs. They were pointed out to me, but I was so overwhelmed just managing her behavior that I didn't see it. If I did, I didn't recognize it for the danger that it presented to her.

Q: Part of it was being overwhelmed, part of it was denial? Is that a fair assessment?

A: I think it is because I didn't realize that she had started to use heroin. I thought it was cigarettes, maybe a little marijuana, a few pills and alcohol. I was almost rationalizing if I saw an empty bottle of liquor or smelled some marijuana on her that, "It's not as bad. It's only that. Thank goodness it's not something stronger or worse." I didn't realize that she was already in the grips of heroin.

Q: What advice would you give to a parent? Obviously, the sooner you deal with the situation realistically, the better off you are. It's normal for a parent to not want to see these things. What would be your two cents to someone about denial and coming to grips with what's really happening?

A: That's a hard one to answer. I think you look at your child through your lens and you don't want to believe it. When you do see it and you know you have to do something, you don't know where to begin and there's that feeling of terror and hopelessness and helplessness. My advice is to use your resources and talk to anyone whether that's a trusted friend, clergy, or a counselor or someone in your child's school ...a teacher or a guidance counselor. I always say you can go to the police because they're open all the time, 24/7.

They don't require a co-payment and they see a lot of this and can often direct you to resources, whether that's the court for a child in need of services or something else. There's a lot of help resources available online, too ...phone calls that you can make, but just start reaching out even if it's hard.

Q: Now, you tell us that Bianca had a mental illness and that she was adopted. Was her biological mother an addict?

A: We have limited information about Bianca's biological parents. When she came to us, it was a closed adoption. What I do know based on just the short time that she had Bianca for those two years is that there was a lot of turmoil and chaos. Her birthmother didn't follow through with the plans for Bianca with the social services piece and as a result, Bianca slipped from her grasp.

I can only assume that she may have suffered some of the same chemical imbalances that Bianca did, given sometimes the strong link between genetics of parent and child. Clearly, Bianca had mental illness so perhaps her mother did as well, but I think Bianca's biology made her adoption more difficult because of the mental illness.

you say to someone who says, "Hey, my
ally ill. My child was not adopted. My
.ıc of years was not chaotic. All this doesn't
..ıe." What would you say to that person?

A: Those factors don't apply to you. When we're dealing
with addiction, there's sometimes no answer as to why it
started. I think for Bianca, it began because she was somehow
broken inside, a little bit, whether that was from her early
years or the mental illness. But addiction, in and of itself, I
don't know. My belief is that there's brokenness somewhere
and drugs are what the person turns to for comfort and help.

Q: What are your thoughts about genetics versus environment
when it comes to addiction? Many would think that if a child
at a young age is given loving parents, warm household,
having a lot of fun and healthy activities available to them,
that those circumstances would prevail over genetics. What
do you think?

A: There was a college professor my husband argued this
very point with when he was studying for his sociology
undergraduate major. He said, "No, it's definitely
environment," and the professor said, "No, it's definitely
genetics." I can see that we gave Bianca every opportunity.
She had a loving family. We were stable financially. We had
a loving marriage. I was basically a stay-at-home mother.
My husband and I both have graduate degrees. We gave
her every opportunity and resource. Her biology kicked in
regardless of what we did. We saw that unfold in front of our
eyes, and we couldn't stop it.

Q: Do you feel there was a stigma attached to you as a parent of an addicted child?

A: There was a stigma attached to me as a parent because my child was so mentally ill first. She became difficult to handle, and her illness spilled out into our neighborhood and community. As I often say, there was no race for the cure or pretty ribbon or any curb appeal for the mental illness that she had. As a result, it was very difficult for other families of school-aged children or children in her class, or children in our neighborhood because they didn't want their children to be around it.

I really couldn't blame them because sometimes her behavior was so outrageous and out of control. They were polite and they did the best they could. We tried to do the best we could, but there was a lot of stigma just parenting someone so desperately ill. Once the addiction became more pronounced and her name was in the newspapers, there was even more shame because she was our child, and the implication was that we may have had a direct or indirect role in this.

Q: How did that affect you, your family, having that stigma or thoughts attached to you?

A: It was humiliating and we've always prided ourselves in being kind, professional, good neighbors and giving to our community. It was really hard to have this child who was so mentally ill, so obviously sick. It impacted our work because we were getting calls at work. It impacted our family. I didn't dare take her places — even into people's homes — because I was afraid she would steal. She did steal from some of our relatives.

It was very hard for my mother, Bianca's grandmother, to see the way that Bianca was treating me. She had a hard time with that, and I think she resented Bianca for it. They never completely reconciled their relationship over the years.

Q: Does that create additional stress for you?

A: It does because it's hard to listen to criticism of your child even though you know there is a basis for it. Bianca was not often nice when she was so ill.

Q: We'll come back to friends and family later on. In the beginning it must be a parent's natural reaction to want to fix it or cure the problem. Was that yours?

A: Yes, it was. Especially when she was in our home, and we were desperately trying to get resources for her. We wanted to fix it so she could be normal and have a normal adolescence. When it became apparent that everything we were doing wasn't helping, that became very hard and we tried to get the resources for her but it wasn't enough. She ended up having to be removed from our home and be contained.

Q: Let's go to the point where you're feeling that it's your responsibility and it's your duty to save Bianca no matter what. Was that your mindset at one point?

A: It was to a point. At some point you have to save yourself. We exhausted ourselves, we put up with a lot because we loved her and we were her parents and tried to do everything possible, but there did come a point where I reached my limit. We were in danger from her and her activities. She

was putting our family at risk, and we had to set a limit —
we had to draw a line in the sand. I finally said, "You can't
live here anymore."

Q: How difficult was it to reach that point where you had
to draw a line in the sand, knowing that there would be
consequences for the child that may not be positive. How
difficult was it to reach that point?

A: Well, it took a long time. It was many years and I didn't
see it coming. I didn't know I had reached my limit until I
was there. She put my son in danger when he was going back
into a war zone in the army. He'd come home on leave and
she'd taken his cell phone with all of his contact information.
I didn't see that line in the sand coming, but there it was
because she had put him in danger and I was protecting him
and my house from her activities, including stealing.

Q: Is there a point where maybe a parent's desire to fix it or
save the child is actually an unhealthy thing? What would
you say to a parent who has to make that decision? When
is wanting to fix things actually an unhealthy thing for the
parent and the child?

A: You have to take care of yourself first. I learned that the
hard way. I let myself and my health suffer because I was
trying so hard. It reminds me of when you are in an airplane,
and the oxygen mask comes down and they tell you to put
your own mask on first and then help others. You can't help
anybody in your family if you're not healthy first. At some
point you have to love yourself more or love yourself first. If
you don't do that, you won't be of any use to anybody else
and you won't be able to help your child.

Q: You're free to make your own decisions about how you're going to live your life. The child is not going to make those decisions.

A: Absolutely.

Q: Now, as the parent of an addicted child you've had to deal with many things. Dishonesty, manipulation, selfishness, theft, guilt, frustration, bad behavior and seeing someone you love make astonishingly bad, self-destructive decisions over and over again — that comes across in the book. It was infuriatingly frustrating to see these things happening. Is there any possible way that you can prepare yourself for that?

A: I think you live in the moment. I don't know if there is a way to prepare for it. You keep swimming. It's the only analogy I can think of. It's almost like when you're treading water and you're holding up one beach ball, and then you begin to hold another, and then another and you're doing the best you can. There is really no way to prepare for that. It's almost as if you're reacting to each event and the cumulative toll over time has its effect on you. You can drown if you don't take care of yourself first.

Q: Let's talk about enabling. Where do you think the line is between helping an addicted child and enabling an addicted child?

A: We struggled with that. I struggled with that because we wanted to help her, especially when we knew that she was out of our home and living on the streets.

There were many times when before she had a permanent place to live — an apartment that we found for her — when she would call and plead for us to take care of her and bring her home. The worry as a parent was if I said no, she'd be on the streets and that's a dangerous place to be. If I'd said yes, then I was at risk of enabling. Every time a parent tries to help a child they have to weigh everything and ask, "Am I helping? Am I enabling? And what is the result of my action? Is it the right one?" Sometimes you never really know.

Q: Do you think there's a point where trying to protect them from the consequences of their actions is actually more of the danger to them than their addiction?

A: For us it was because, in retrospect, every time she got in trouble we would bail her out because we were worried that she would have a record. We tried to help her by connecting her with counselors and bringing her to appointments that she couldn't have attended if she were in jail. So, we enabled her. If we hadn't bailed her out, she would have gone to jail. When she eventually did go to jail, it was a positive experience in that she was safe, she was off the streets, she wasn't using, and she began real work. She attended the Narcotics Anonymous meetings that were held at the jail as well as some vocational training and worked on her GED. Jail wasn't as bad an experience as we thought it would be.

Q: Trying to save them from the consequences of their decisions is not always a positive thing.

A: True, that's true.

Q: Are there lessons you think they have to learn themselves?

A: Yes, there are. It was when we involved the courts and the probation officers and had some weight behind our parental authority. That was a lesson that Bianca learned, and I remember telling her that if she continued with her behavior she was going to be further and further away from the family. She looked right at me and said, "I don't care." That moment when the court said you will behave and you will do these things, and you will go to school she realized that if she didn't do those things she would be in the land of "I don't care" and would be further and further away from the people she loved and who loved her.

Q: That leads us to the issue of boundaries. Related to being supportive and yet not enabling is the issue of boundaries. How important is it to set boundaries?

A: It's vital. Without clear boundaries you can't help yourself.

Your child has no structure, no way to be contained, and no safety. You must be in charge. You have to be the parent. We tried to do that. I think we did a good job considering what we were faced with. We were a united front, my husband and me. We set boundaries which were vital to keep our sanity, to keep our household running and to keep our family intact.

Q: Can you give us some examples of the boundaries you set along the way?

A: There were boundaries with her behavior, starting when she was little. We did the timeouts, of course, for the bad behavior and the explanation. Boundaries became more challenging when she got older and was so mentally ill because you weren't sure after a while. I don't know if it was the sleep deprivation, not knowing what was real and what wasn't and struggling to set boundaries. Sometimes you feel the boundaries may be a little too little and too late. But they are vital. You don't always do well setting them clearly, because you're living in the midst of such chaos and turmoil. So, you just do the best you can. But yes, they are important.

Q: It must be very hard to be consistent with boundaries. How important is it to be consistent?

A: Oh, it's very important to be consistent. But, again, I don't think we were. I tried as hard as I could, but I was probably inconsistent at times. In the moment I thought I was doing the best that I could. But in retrospect, the boundaries I set could have been clearer and sharper. I was living the experience with my addicted, mentally ill daughter, and sometimes those boundaries got blurred.

Q: It must not be easy to stick to boundaries. When you did stick to them, in the book you talk about being met with ferocious opposition and attacks. I think many parents end up just giving in. What do you say to a parent who's under attack and flirting with the idea of just giving in to get some relief from the abuse?

A: If you give in, it'll continue. It needs to be contained. When I did set those limits, it was to preserve myself. Sometimes they were set out of frustration, and in the moment when

I was reacting to some outrageous behavior. But without boundaries, your addicted child has no way to be contained.

Q: Can you expand on this a little more? Your concept of boundaries is great. But then when you're faced with the reality of sticking to the boundary, your child goes to jail. You think, "My child may not have a place to live tonight. My child might be in an unsafe situation." Can you tell us a little bit more about how difficult it was to do that? And what compelled you to stick to your guns?

A: It's terrifying. When setting those boundaries, if it means that your child is now homeless, or that your child is going to jail, or they're hungry or they're whatever. If you don't stick to the boundaries you've set, you'll drown, too. You won't be safe. For me, it was about my safety. The times when I set the boundaries, it was because I had to retain the sanctity of my home by keeping my family safe, and keeping myself safe. I loved our daughter, but I had to love myself first.

Q: I read somewhere that to help an addicted loved one, you have to say what you mean, mean what you say, but don't say it mean. What does that mean to you?

A: That's true. When I look back now and examine how I parented Bianca, one thing I did right was to follow through with what I said to the best of my ability. But I tried not to say anything to her in anger or from a place of wanting to get back at her. I did lose my temper on occasion and one time she put my son in danger by stealing his cell phone. For the most part, I consciously made every interaction honest, truthful and kind. I tried to be kind and fair. Years later, she said to me, "Thank you, mommy, for never calling me an addict."

And it would've been easy to do that. It's easy to fight blow for blow, fight fire with fire. If you're attacked, it's easy to lash out. When you love your child, and we all do love our children, and they're so ill, you have to step back and realize that it's the illness that's taken over. And you can't be mean to illness. They're sick, they're desperately sick. If you react in kind, and you're mean back, or you're angry back, it'll make things a lot worse.

Q: Can you share a little more about how you communicated with Bianca in terms of the way you would talk to her? Maybe words or phrases that you would avoid. You describe in the book how you walked on eggshells. Give us some hints on how to communicate with someone with an addiction.

A: That's a great question. During my training to become a nurse, I learned techniques on how to deal with psychiatric patients. And I used those tools all the time when I was dealing with Bianca and raising her. The first thing is to use I-statements instead of you-statements. For example, I never said, "You make me..." or, "You are . . . " and label it. I would say instead, "I am unhappy when...," or "What you did affected me this way." It tried to communicate from a place of understanding. I didn't want to attack her and point a finger.

I would reflect and say to her, "This is what I'm seeing. This is how it's affecting me. This is why it's not acceptable. This is what I'm going to do. This is what I expect." It put the conversation and the limit setting in a different place but it also enraged her. Many times she was so angry, she wanted to get me to react, and she was looking for a fight. And when I didn't give it to her, that frustration really had nowhere to go.

Q: What else can you tell us about communication styles?

A: Sometimes it's easier to walk away. Or, actually, sometimes it's harder to walk away, depending on the situation.

Q: Pick your battles?

A: Yes. Pick your battles, pick your fights. There were times when I wanted to stop the behavior, but it wasn't worth the effort, because I had a bigger battle to fight. Was it always worthwhile to get angry when she left a huge mess in the kitchen? That's one example. Sometimes it was, sometimes it wasn't. Perhaps there were other things that were more important. Maybe that day she needed to take a bath. Or that day she was going to an appointment. That was what I put my energy into. Or I had something in my own life that I had to deal with.

Q: Regarding your comment about how Bianca would try to make you angry, it's very evident that you and your husband, Karl, gave so much again and again, and yet were pushed away; rejected by someone you loved very much while you desperately wanted to help. How does anyone handle that kind of rejection?

A: When it comes from your child, it's devastating. It hurts very much. There isn't a good way to handle it. I think you have to have a good healthy respect for yourself and your self-worth and draw your strength from whatever sources you can. For us, it was our strong marriage, it was our family and friends and it was our faith. That's what gets you through. Because it's very unpleasant, and it hurts.

Q: Let's talk some about treatment in rehab. Many parents seem to think that treatment or rehab is going to be a cure. Is it a cure? And what would be reasonable expectations for the process of treatment and rehabilitation?

A: With treatment, there is always hope that the person will get better. Bianca never went into a drug treatment program unfortunately. When she became mentally ill, treatment focused on stabilizing and containing her mental illness. In that environment, she did well. The drama was removed, and she recovered in a safe, contained place. So, in that respect, her mental illness was managed successfully when she was in a treatment program.

I wonder if she had gone into an addiction treatment program, would it have made a difference in her life. We were trying to get her into a program right up until she died. She met with a counselor and had an appointment with a primary care physician. These were prerequisites for psychiatric care and prescriptions. It looked like she was doing well. She was saying and doing all the right things, but she was still using heroin. As a parent, you can only do so much - put programs or resources in place. It's up to the individual to decide whether they're going to use them or not.

Q: What pointers would you give to a parent in dealing with the various treatment teams? In your book, it seems that overall you were very grateful to most of the people who tried to help you. In some instances where you didn't seem to think people were being helpful or realistic, what advice would you pass on in terms of dealing with people helping a child with treatment?

A: You must realize that the professionals are working on behalf of your child. You can't relinquish all the responsibility to them, as good as they are. It is a team effort, and they offer specific supports and have certain objectives. I put my ego aside and worked with them. It was not always easy. They may challenge you, or they may do things differently, or they may ask for your help in ways that force you to look at issues and confront the illness.

Q: The title of your book 'Addict Behind Our Bedroom Door' - what were you hoping that would convey?

A: I struggled with the title. There were so many times when we were afraid for ourselves and afraid for our daughter. What I try to convey in the book title is that we never felt safe; her addiction never left us. The addiction followed us into our bedroom, in the most sacred place in our home. We locked our doors many nights, because we were afraid that if we didn't, the mental illness and addiction would come into our bedroom. Even with the door locked, it intruded, whether it was the noise, or the cooking smells or people coming into our home. As a family, and as a couple, and as individuals, we weren't safe. I wasn't safe, and the addiction was always present and very dangerous.

Q: Dealing with fear, as you mentioned, the details you share are many times quite scary. Not only for the circumstances Bianca put herself into, but you and Karl had things to fear

- not being safe in your home, being attacked physically and being falsely accused of things by a child manipulating the system. When did you really start to feel a deep fear?

A: There were several times when I felt deep fear. The first was when she threatened to falsely accuse me. I was afraid again when the addiction came into our home. Bianca was bringing people that we didn't know into our house. The type of people you see hanging around street corners - most undesirable. I was also afraid when she stole from me and our family. I was afraid of her behavior when she was high. I was afraid of the illegal activities that were happening because of her addiction. I was afraid because I didn't know who had access to our home. I didn't know if she'd given people copies of our house key. I was afraid all the time.

After she moved out, and actually while she was in jail, we sold our house and we moved to a new home. No one had keys but us. That's how I began to feel safe again. But there were many years when I feared I would be killed or that some great harm would come to me or my family.

Q: Guilt. It's very normal for a parent to feel guilty in this situation, guilty of some things. But someone who has an addiction also uses guilt as a weapon to get what they want, as you've mentioned. How do you handle that?

A: I think there's always guilt. You're guilty that you did too much; you're guilty that you didn't do enough. In the end, now that she's dead, I struggle with guilt. I feel that her death was a failure in many respects because she no longer had a chance. Who failed her? Did we fail her? Did the system fail her? Did society fail her? These unanswered questions cause struggles with guilt. You want to do more but you have to preserve yourself. There's a balance. You're never sure if it's the right balance. Help them, help yourself, set a boundary, move the boundary a little bit, be flexible, be kind, be tough, be strong. These are polarities you're juggling all the time, and the result of that is guilt. You just have to know in your heart that you tried. "I think for me I did the best I could."

Q: Do you think you'll ever be able to let the guilt go?

A: I hope so. It's not easy, holding it. It's easy to cling to guilt, to be angry, to say, "Why did this happen? What did I do? How could I have prevented it?" And sometimes there are no answers, and that's the struggle.

Q: You mentioned earlier about dealing with family members, and you mentioned friends. Parents of addicted children often say it's very hard to speak to family and friends about their child's addiction. What advice would you give to someone?

A: There were family and friends we could talk freely with and get support from. But they were few, not a lot. Because I don't think people in general, and some of our family and friends in particular, were comfortable. They were judging through their lens what our situation was. I think there was a lot of misunderstanding. I also think they were afraid of Bianca, and they were afraid for us but they didn't know what to do. My advice is, even if you don't know what to do when you know someone you care about has to deal with an addicted child or family member, just listen, be there and try to help.

Q: Well-meaning friends and family probably have no real concept of the totality of what's going on, and you mentioned getting advice from certain family members. How did you react to advice from friends and family?

A: It was interesting. Because one of my dear friends worked as a psychiatric nurse. And she saw the danger that we were in years before we realized how bad it was. She was always concerned for our safety. She would give loving advice and recommendations, and I didn't believe her. So, that was one example. And then sometimes there were well-meaning family members who would give advice, but they didn't have a clue what we were dealing with. We tried to protect people because for the sake of our boys and our family we wanted to have it be as normal as possible.

In some ways, we weren't as honest as we could have been. We were doing the best we could, but we were pretending sometimes that things were better than they really were because we didn't want to worry anybody.

Q: Your book is unique as it gives a very detailed blow-by-blow account of what it's like. It's an eye opener for friends, or siblings, or grandparents to read about what might be going on, but who may have no clue. What do you hope that friends, siblings or grandparents learn from your book?

A: I think that when you love someone, and they have an addicted child, the reason that the addiction is happening is no fault of the parents. There's a lot of hidden drama and trauma that you may not always be aware of, so I tried to show the raw reality of living with mental illness day in and day out, year after year, as a basis for understanding that it's no one's fault. Everyone's doing the best they can in a sometimes impossible situation. Maybe there would be just some understanding and a little kindness that would go along with the worry that you would have for the family while they're dealing with this.

Q: A child's addiction puts a strain on relationships, finances and careers. Many parents who've had to deal with this have seen their marriages fail and finances in ruin. Can you share your thoughts about doing everything you can to help your child without sacrificing your own happiness and future?

A: I think it would have been very easy for Karl and me to point a finger at each other and blame. We made a purposeful decision and a consistent commitment almost on a daily basis to work together. We had an agreement that if one of us felt strongly about an issue, more strongly than the other, that we would agree to disagree, but we would go with whichever parent felt more strongly about an issue. That act gave us a united front against the children when they acted out or acted against us. We always took time to do something fun, even if it was going out for a slice of pizza. We spent a lot of time just walking and talking.

I think the key for us, and perhaps for other marriages is to just take time to be together. You might discuss the children, but you limit the amount of time you talk about them, and then you talk about other things. We never blamed each other for Bianca's behavior.

Q: In your book, you described the tremendous effort you made to help Bianca do the right thing. Can you expand a little bit more about the time it takes parents to make sure they're okay? What amount of work has to be done? I'm going to assume it's not by accident that you come through this storm okay. What should a couple expect to help them come through this?

A: I think taking time for each other, and taking time for you is the answer. It's hard to do when you're in the midst of it, and you don't always do it well. But getting enough sleep, eating right, not drinking a lot, not popping pills and other crutches make it easier. I think you have to have faith that you will get through it. I think you have to have faith that you're not alone, that people care about you, and there are people who will help your child. But you have to take the time to put your marriage first and help stabilize the family through that united front.

Q: What would you say to someone who thinks it's selfish to think like that when a child's addicted?

A: It is a little selfish, but if you're not selfish, you won't be available for your child or yourself. You end up with no energy, no resources and no time left to take care of anyone. That's the message. You have to love yourself first and then love your child.

Q: Are there any questions I have not asked that you wish I had?

A: I think readers might ask if I'd do it again. Was it worth it to parent Bianca? There are times when I thought it wasn't and that I would never do it again if you paid me millions of dollars. But being two-and-a-half years past her death, I do think that it was worth it. She was, underneath it all, a kind person, and there were many times even in the midst of her addiction when she was kind and full of life. Those are the moments when it was worth it. I'll give you an example. After she passed away, one of her friends who was also an addict and had been in and out of jail called and put a plea out in the middle of the night. It was the bitter cold in January, he had no place to stay, and he was looking for a place to crash. He told us afterwards, after Bianca's passing, that she was the only friend at 2 a.m. who said, "You come here. There's warm food for you. Friends don't let friends stay out in the cold alone." I'm happy that we raised her to be kind. It's sad that she is gone and I miss her, but we did the best we could, and it was because we loved her no matter what.

Q: In summary, could you pass along some advice to parents who are facing these issues?

A: You're doing the best you can, and you'll never know if it's enough. You just have to put one foot in front of the other each day and try to take care of yourself. Never give up hope and never stop loving or living your life.

ABOUT
the author

D. L. Wilson grew up in the hills
and valleys of western Massachusetts.
She moved to Massachusetts' North Shore
to study nursing and received both
her Bachelor of Science and Master of Science
nursing degrees. With 36 years of experience
as a Registered Nurse, D.L. is board certified
in rehabilitation nursing. D.L. has worked
as a Visiting Guest Lecturer and
Clinical Faculty and is employed as
a Clinical Nurse Specialist.
She and her husband Karl live quietly
on the Massachusetts coast and enjoy
walking on the beach and
spending time with their sons.

Promise
Me
Please

Promise me you will stay forever
Promise me you will never go
Promise me you will get better
Promise you will follow through.

Promise your life is precious
Promise to stop this madness
Promise to battle your demons
I promise to fight the war with you.

Promise your life has meaning
Promise your words are true
Promise you believe in something
Promise to keep a promise, as I always promise you.

Promise this grief will leave me
Promise the pain will ease
Promise you are well now
Promise me, oh promise me please.

By D.L. Wilson
in Loving Memory of Bianca Wilson

The Wilson Family

D.L., Bianca, Karl, Stephen, Michael

More photos at:
DLWilsonWrites.com

RESOURCES

211 Information and Referral Search
Phone: 211. www.211.org. Dial 2-1-1 for free and confidential information and referral information regarding help with food, housing, employment, health care, and counseling.

AIDS Action Committee
Phone: (877) 627-3933 (toll-free sexual health helpline for young adults) phone: (877) 232-4636 (toll-free HIV/AIDS and Hepatitis C hotline). www. aac.org www.mariatalks.com. Helpline and website for information about sexuality, STDs, birth control, emergency contraception, and parenting. Alternative House. Phone: (978) 454-1436 toll-free: (888) 291-6228. www. alternative-house.org. 24-hour crisis hotline for victims of domestic violence. Provides resources and information regarding medical, psychiatric, legal and housing matters.

The ANSWER BOOK
www.masscip.org/youthresources. A website with information for adolescents and young adults under the care or custody of or working with the Department of Children and Families. For a hard copy, contact the Children's Law Center.

Autism Speaks
www.autismspeaks.org/resource-guide/state/MA. A guide to resources for youth with autism and their families.

Blueskies Wellness, Inc.
Phone: (888) 336-1411. blueskieswellnessinc.org. Confidential anti-bullying help for kids 13 years old and older.

Boston Area Rape Crisis Center (BARCC)
Phone: (800) 841-8371 Spanish: (800) 223-5001. www.barcc.org. Statewide hotline to assist survivors of rape.

RESOURCES

Child at Risk Hotline (DCF 24-Hour Hotline)
Phone: (617) 232-4882 toll-free: (800) 792-5200. Free, 24/7 after-hours
emergency response system providing crisis intervention, information,
or referrals for children in danger.

Children's Law Center of Massachusetts
Phone: (781) 581-1977 toll-free: (888) KIDLAW8 or (888) 543-5298.
Provides information, referrals, and/or legal advice
on matters that impact children.

Department of Corrections Victim Services Unit
Phone: (866) 6VICTIM or (866) 684-2846. Domestic violence helpline.

Federation for Children with Special Needs
Parental Training and Information Center
Phone: (617) 236-7210 toll-free: (800) 331-0688. www.fcsn.org/ptic. Hours:
M–F 10–3. Confidential helpline answering questions
about special education.

Gay, Lesbian, Bisexual, and Transgender National Hotline National
Hotline Phone: (888) 843-4564 Youth Talk line: (800) 246-7743. Hours: M–F
4–12; Sat 12–5. www.youthtalkline.org. Provides telephone and email peer-
counseling, as well as factual information and local resources
for cities and towns across the United States.

GLBTQ Domestic Violence Project hotline
Phone: (800) 832-1901 Helpline: (617) 779-2127 (sexual assault helpline).
www.glbtqdvp.org. Provides free and confidential support and services for
GLBTQ survivors of domestic and sexual violence.

Healing Abuse Working for Change (HAWC)
Phone: (800) 547-1649 TTY: (978) 744-1818. www.hawcdv.org.
Abuse hotline provides 24-hour assistance.

RESOURCES

Health Care for All
Phone: (800) 272-4232. www.hcfama.org. Provides information about
health care and assists at-risk individuals obtain health insurance coverage.

Jane Doe Inc.
Phone: (877) 785-2020. www.janedoe.org. Domestic violence helpline.

Legal Advocacy and Resource Center (LARC)
Hotline phone: (617) 603-1700 toll-free: (800) 342-5297. Hours: M–F 9–1
Languages: English, Spanish, Portuguese Hotline to assist
individuals with legal problems.

Massachusetts Advocates for Children
Phone: (617) 357-8431 ext 224. www.massadvocates.org. Provides
helpline assistance to children who are experiencing barriers to education
due to disabilities, homelessness, suspension,
expulsion, or domestic violence.

Massachusetts Behavioral Health Access
www.mabhaccess.com. Website with information about MassHealth
providers of behavioral health services searchable by geographic area.
Provides information about waiting times. Login as a "Guest".

Massachusetts Department of Public Health (DPH)
Community Support Line
Phone (800) 882-1435. Informs families with children with special health
needs about public programs and benefits they may be eligible for, and
about the state and community-based resources
that may provide assistance.

Massachusetts Legal Websites Project
www.masslegalhelp.org. Legal information written by lawyers
for non-lawyers on a variety of topics.

RESOURCES

Massachusetts Office for Victim Assistance (MOVA)
Phone: (617) 586-1340. www.mass.gov/mova.
Offers a variety of resources for victims of crime.

National Alliance on Mental Illness (NAMI) Helpline
Phone: (800) 950-NAMI. www.nami.org. Hours: M–F 10–6.
Provides assistance to those affected by mental illness.

National Domestic Violence Hotline
Phone: (800) 656-SAFE (7233) TTY: (800) 787-3224. www.thehotline.org.
National helpline for victims of domestic violence.

The Network/La Red
Phone: (617) 742-4911. www.tnlr.org. Hotline providing support,
information, and safety planning for lesbian, gay, bisexual, and/or
transgender (LGBQ/T) folk experiencing or having experienced abuse.

Parents Helping Parents - Parental Stress Line
Phone: (800) 632-8188. www.parentshelpingparents.org.
Toll-free confidential helpline providing support for parents.

Project Bread Food Source Hotline
Phone: (800) 645-8333 Hours: M–F 8–7; Sat 10–2. 60+ languages. Hotline
to refer callers to emergency food resources in their community.

Rape, Abuse, & Incest National Network (RAINN)
Phone: (800) 656-4673 ext 1. www.rainn.org.
National helpline for victims of sexual abuse.

Substance Abuse and Mental Health
Services Administration (SAMHSA)
National Helpline Phone (800) 662-HELP (4357). www.samhsa.gov.
Confidential, free, 24/7 helpline available in Spanish and English.
Provides referrals to local supports.
Callers can also order free publications and other information.

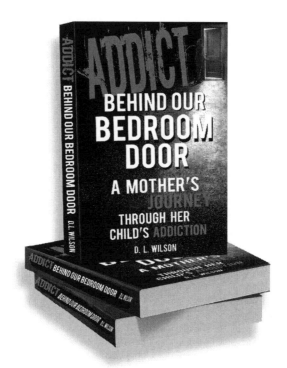

This book is available at quantity discounts for bulk purchases.

Inquire at
DLWilsonWrites.com

D.L. Wilson Speaks.

Have D.L. present at your next event or organizational meeting.

Inquire at DLWilsonWrites.com

Made in the USA
Columbia, SC
25 April 2018